NO
BULL***T

NO
BULL***T

Lyn Partridge-Webber. Wellington Witch

authorHOUSE®

AuthorHouse™ UK
1663 Liberty Drive
Bloomington, IN 47403 USA
www.authorhouse.co.uk
Phone: 0800.197.4150

Published by AuthorHouse 01/20/2015

ISBN: 978-1-5049-3588-3 (sc)
ISBN: 978-1-5049-3589-0 (e)

Contents

When people meet a medium, they think he or she can read their mind and know everything about them. Others think mediums know all the answers to their problems. Again this is untrue. We are just ordinary people having experiences in this world to progress our soul, this is part of my journey.

www.wellingtonwitch.co.uk

Chapter One

Things were never going to be the same again

The evening started much the same as any other Monday at circle, with a meditation. As soon as I closed my eyes, I became aware of my Native American guide, he was surrounded by many other Native American's. One stepped forward as if acting as a spokesperson, he told me he was Sitting Bull, a name I had heard many times but had no idea what he looked like before now. He told me that the earth was going to go through many changes in the next few years, and encouraged me to tell as many people as possible through modern media that these changes were coming. I asked what changes these were. Earth is fast approaching 21.12.2012 he said and before that, many people were needed to help to make these changes possible. He told me that these people had volunteered to be on earth during this important time, many had forgotten their mission and it was time for people to wake up and remember why they were here.

I had of course been aware of 21.12.2012 being an important date, I had been told over fifty years before by my spirit guides that this would be the start of a new golden age on earth which would last 2000 years, I was also told that we would not be allowed to destroy the earth with nuclear weapons as many other planets would be affected. So through the nuclear crisis in the 1960's and many times after that, I have held onto that information which has given me peace of mind in very difficult times. During the 1960's the age of "make love not war" the swinging 60's music scene, hippies beatniks and a feeling of complete happiness, I have always thought, if this is what2012 is going to be like, bring it on, it will be such a good time.

So why was I being told about the need to tell as many people as possible? I didn't understand at all. All too soon it was time to come back from the meditation, we usually share anything interesting that the spirit world tell us and I was eager to share what I had been told! So imagine my surprise when the first lady to speak said, "I have been told by Geronimo, that I have to tell people of earth about changes coming." Almost all the circle had a similar message, the only thing that differed was who bought that information, some saw Geronimo, some Red Cloud, and some like me, saw sitting bull. The rest of the evening was taken up with what we had been told and how to get this information "out there" Not many people had a laptop or tablet then, most didn't even have a mobile phone, so we decided to write to a newspaper especially aimed at spiritualists and people interested in spiritual messages, which is called the psychic news. Later on that evening I typed out a letter and posted it to the psychic news. After about a week I had two replies from circles that had similar messages to us, one was in Spain and one in Wiltshire in UK. The circle leader from Wiltshire phoned me and asked if we could meet up to discuss the message? I agreed and I and a friend had an enjoyable afternoon exchanging news and information with this lady who has worked with Sitting Bull as a spirit guide for many years. We all agreed to keep in touch and to pass on any other messages any of us received.

A few months later on the July Esbat (full moon) my friend and I decided to travel to Avebury which is a famous stone circle site in the UK, it was about 130 miles from where we lived so we made an early start to have a whole day there. The day was spent sitting close to the stones, meditating, chatting to other visitors and a lunch at the local pub. During the day we climbed to the top of Silbury Hill which is close by and saw a beautiful crop circle in the field below. We also tuned in to the Mary and Michael Ley lines that run through the stone circles and followed them as they weaved in and out of the stones. It was a lovely day and after the sun set above the stones; we waited to see a huge full moon rise above the hill above us. We could hear the singing of a few local witches, hidden by the trees, their voices adding to the lovely peaceful atmosphere.

Soon we saw a few other people arriving, some carrying blankets, and small chairs, obviously they intended to sit in the moonlight and take in the energy of the stone circle. I suddenly noticed the lady leading the circle was the same one who had come to visit me and talk about the messages received from Sitting Bull, she invited us to join her group, and we sat with them for several hours before we travelled home.

Chapter Two
More visits to Avebury

A year passed and as the July Sebat came and went, I asked my friend if she felt she would like to go to Amesbury again as we had the year before? I told her I felt as if I was being told to go. She said she also had this feeling so we set off to visit Amesbury again as we had one year earlier but this time for the August full moon. There seemed to be a lot of people around this year, the group we had joined the previous year were there and felt that they were being drawn there on this special night. Later as the moon rose, there was a large group of people present, people from many parts of the world, all drawn there to be on Avebury on this night, even though no one had contacted anyone else, we had just turned up and it felt right? One of the people there was a Native American in full dress; he played a flute and sang many songs in his own language, and explained the songs and prayers had been passed down through his family. He gave us all a blessing and joined us in our meditation. We all had candles lit and it looked spectacular to see all the lights glowing in the darkness.

As we meditated together, the energy grew stronger and some people started channelling their own spirit guides and passing on messages to us. All of the messages seemed to carry similar prophesies, the earth was going through a huge change, many changes to climate and lands would follow. Much water would come to earth as if a cleansing to help the earth to ascend to the higher vibrations, the earth herself would shudder and shake as she ascended, there would be many lands lost to earthquake and flood. There would be much volcanic activity. Mother earth loves us and wants to take as many of the animal and human life as possible with her into the new age, so she would ascend as gently as she could. As we heard these messages, I was a bit worried, as it seemed to herald doom and gloom. My spirit guides gently reminded me of their original message that we were entering a new golden age in 2012 and many changes were taking place, nothing would ever be the same again . . . . But not to worry, all would happen, as it should. I had heard that before and it usually meant I should worry! The last message I heard from the group was intriguing, it said that before the end of the month, a flower goddess, much loved on earth would be leaving and going back to spirit. She would be much missed and her passing would be spoken of all around the world. As the world took a short intake of breath as they heard the news, it would be like for a fraction of a second, that the earth would seem to stand still, that would be the time when a new vibration would enter the earth and the changes would start to begin.

Roger and I had planned to get married on September 6th and were arranging for this day. Like many other people we were shocked to awake a week before this date, to hear the news that Diana, Princess of Wales had been killed in a car crash in Paris. No one could really believe it had happened and the out pouring of grief all around the world was something not seen on that scale before. I was reminded of the words heard at Amesbury that as people stopped to take a short sharp intake of breath when they heard the news; a new vibration would enter the earth.

Lots of people cancelled their plans for September 6th as it was Diana's funeral, shops were closed, and the towns were very quiet as people stayed at home to watch the day on television. We carried on with our plans to get married and travelled to Paris for a few days afterwards. We stayed a few hours in London and saw the huge amounts of flowers placed in so many places in memory of Diana. It was indeed a huge outpouring of grief that I had not seen before.

Chapter Three

Starting to see and feel the changes

Around this time I ran one circle on Mondays, we had about 12 members, suddenly lots more people became interested in spiritual development, and as I had no more room to accommodate new members, I started a second circle. This also filled up quickly and I was surprised we seemed to be getting a lot more men attending circle recently and had a 50/50 balance of men and woman. Time moved on and as a circle we had lots of good messages and information from the spirit world. Slowly we managed to piece together that Earth had started the move into the new age in 1987 but things had speeded up now, which was ten years later. It was about now that I became aware of the turquoise coloured chakra between the throat and heart especially prominent on men, that I was told was for balance between the male and female energies, as we were rapidly approaching the new age of Aquarius which is a feminine age. We were now nearing the end of Pisces a masculine age. Up until this time most men didn't show their emotions easily, as the new age was going to be an age of love and light, the opening of this chakra would help them to understand that its fine to show emotion, it doesn't make them look weak. It allows them to show their feelings and really be them selves

As a circle we were learning much more about the Pleiades and other star systems, many said they felt an affinity to the Pleiades and felt somehow it was home. One number that occurred many times in people's meditations was 144.000, we didn't understand what it meant some thought it referred to a frequency, others that it was the number of people who were needed to wake up and become light workers. The mystery went on for many years and didn't become clear until after 2012, when I asked spirit about it, I got the usual answer that I would know when I was able to understand. We have recently heard that it's part of the reawakening on the 12 strands of DNA and the activation of the crystal grid, this is still very much in the early stages, but at least we have some understanding of the number now.

Other things were happening as well, one of them was a set of symptoms that people were experiencing, and they included, severe headaches that didn't respond to pain killers, painful teeth, a feeling of tingling especially at night up and down the spine and in the feet. There was also the fatigue, a feeling of extreme tiredness, little did we know that this was one thing that was to continue and get much worse. Another thing that sent a lot of people rushing off to see their doctor was the rapid heartbeat, people were sure they had heart disease or were having a heart attack, most even had EEG tests to check their heart only to be told that there was nothing wrong with them. I wonder if the health service were wondering why so many people were having these strange symptoms when nothing physically could be found. By far the worst at this time was the food sensitivities, food we had always liked and eaten, suddenly started to upset us, especially bread and dairy products. This wouldn't have been of any importance if it was one or two people, but it was more than a coincidence that 11 out of 12 circle members were experiencing these symptoms which lasted about 3-6 weeks on average. Gradually we found out that spiritual people all over the world were feeling these symptoms which had been called the Shambhala symptoms. The food sensitivities seemed to last for months or years for some people but the aches and pains passed after a few weeks.

It was a t this time that spirit told me that the herbs Valerian and Fenugreek would be useful to ease some of these symptoms and that in the future we would be using something called vibrational medicine more. I had never heard of this and asked more. They told me that simply by saying the name of Valerian and Fenugreek, we would get the energy needed to help us from the vibration of the word. Sounded all too far-fetched for me at that time, so I filed it away somewhere in the mass of "might be useful" information I hang on to.

Once while on holiday in India, I had a very rapid heartbeat and felt quite unwell, of course I was worried, suddenly a lady from spirit appeared, I had never seen her before or again afterwards. She appeared to be around 50 years old, had straight fair hair with a band around her head which had a large crystal over the third eye, she wore a light coloured loose robe, she looked kind, but concerned, and told me firmly, don't drop back, whatever you do, don't drop back, keep moving forwards towards the light. My own guides told me afterwards this was because of a change in the vibration within my body and other things like this would happen again in the future.

Life was far from simple now, we all seemed to be rushing about working and by the time we had finished our chores, we had no time to ourselves, quite a few of my friends were splitting up and blaming it on the fact they didn't seem to have any time to devote to each other. Other people were devoting more time to their relationship and family, this meant they were not giving 100% to their work, some were losing their jobs, and others lost their business and went bankrupt. What was happening?

As we approached the year 2000 attention was placed on what would happen when we left 1999 at midnight 31st December, would the world computers crash, people were worried that aeroplanes losing all their instruments and the financial complications of countries not being in contact with each other. The doom mongers were predicting the end of the world, some were predicting months of darkness upon the earth. There was a lot of panic about. I had several people just knock on my door and ask if it really was the end of the world. All I could say was that it was the end of an age coming up, not the end of the world. Although that world may not be the one they were used to. Of course 2000 dawned and all was OK, the world hadn't come to an end and for the majority of people all seemed to be the same as ever and except for the feeling of time rushing on, lots of people were unaware of the rapidly approaching 2012 or the changes which were expected to happen on 21.12.2012

Chapter Four

Harry Potter films encourage me to talk about witchcraft

For me, one of the biggest changes was the release of the Harry Potter films. Apart from being extremely successful, they bought witchcraft back into the public eye. Everywhere seemed to be either advertising the films or books, many products appeared in the shops, some spell books became very easy to buy. The main worry I had with this was people might dabble with magic without knowing anything about it, no guidance, no protection, and no real understanding. This worried me as a witch a lot. I had never really shared my connection with witchcraft with anyone. People knew me as a medium and secretary of the spiritualist church but knew little of my private life with witchcraft. Eventually I decided to offer very basic guidelines to anyone interested in finding out more about witchcraft and how to work with it safely. The local newspapers started referring to me as Wellington Witch and it stuck. When the first Harry Potter film was showing in our town, a band of concerned people decided to protest, the walked up and down the street outside the local cinema which was close to where I lived, with large signs saying, don't let your children see Harry potter, it will lead them into black Magic.

A TV crew were sent to film the protest and speak to the protesters about their fear, and then they came to speak to me and asked, what does a real witch think about the Harry Potter films? I told them that I was just an ordinary person, with an ordinary life and thought the film carried the message that Love conquers all; it was about good triumphing over evil. As the TV cameras panned around my house with the crystal balls, candles, pentagrams, many spiritual pictures, incense smoke and Ferdinand, my bulls skull on the wall, I thought how absurd it sounded saying I am just the same as anyone else. And had a little smile at how my unusual living room would look on TV. The reporter asked if it was true that Harry potter rode his broomstick the wrong way round, should he ride with the brush to the front or the back, I smiled and told him, actually we don't really ride on broomsticks!

Life became very busy with TV appearances, radio chat shows and many magazine and newspaper articles.

Chapter Five

Important dates and the universal time clock

Years earlier when I had first become interested in 2012, I was told that according to the Universal time clock, we take 26.000 to cover a quarter of a clock face, so a full circle of a clock, four quarters would be 104.000 years and on 21.12.12 not only would we be at the end of Pisces(a masculine age) and going into Aquarius,(a feminine age) we were also at 12.00pm, which was the end of a whole turn of the universal clock 104,000 years, a very important time for all on Earth. The Mayan whose calendars didn't go beyond 21.12.2012, also the Aborigine's, Native American and the Egyptians who all spoke of the end of the world on that date knew this. This was taken as literal by many but I know it refers to the end of the world as we know it.

Many years ago, I had read an article about the Schumann resonance which is also called the heartbeat of the earth; it's a natural rhythm and has been 7.5 for thousands of years. Scientists were saying that after 1987 that they had proof that the Schumann resonance was indeed speeding up and was measuring 9.5. During a meditation we were told that the increase would give the impression of time speeding up, so although we still had 24 hours in a day according to our clocks, the sun still rose, and set the same, we had in fact lost 6 hours off a day. This would mean that we were trying to fit in all the things we had ever done but in 18 hours. So if we put all put all our time into our job, our relationship suffered, if we put all the time into our relationship, our work and jobs suffered, we were in fact chasing our tail from morning till night. Over the coming years the Schumann resonance was measured at 12.12, the scientists said that 13 heralded a pole flip. A lot of people find this hard to believe and many theories were put forward to either try to prove or make sense of how time can be speeding up? One interesting theory one of the men in circle came to was, he liked his eggs boiled for three minutes, and they were perfect and just how he liked them. Recently at three minutes they were not cooked at all properly and he said this was his proof that time really has speeded up.

We know there is no time in the spirit world and that many people choose to live a life on earth to experience time. We are used to the earth being in the third dimension and all that goes with that. There was a lot of confusion what was happening to earth and if she would ascend to the 4th or 5th dimension? Some people thought that there is so much dark negative energy on earth that she would have to go to the 5th dimension to be free of it; others thought that would be impossible. It was sure going to be interesting to see what the future would hold for us all.

Chapter Six
More travelling tales

I was still enjoying travelling around the world when I could so maybe this is the time to share a few more travelling tales to lighten up a bit? People often ask where is my favourite place out of all the ones I have visited so far. Number one is Arizona; two is Thailand and three, The Isle of Skye. The first time I visited Skye I was intrigued by the ruggedness of the landscape, the friendliness of the locals and of course the compete acceptance of witches. After spending two weeks in Skye many years ago, I decided I wasn't going back home. I was offered a job and all set to stay there until one night I had a visit from the spirit of a local witch, she told me I had free will and could stay on Skye, and, was I sure this was my destiny? I told her I had no idea what my destiny was. She told me to think long and hard. I thought back over my time there. The past few weeks had been very hectic, spending every night in the pub or visiting local families, I had a ball. I have many memories of my times in Skye, one being after a heavy night in a local pub, I started my car up ready to drive back to where I was staying, suddenly I saw a man who was much the worse for wear after sampling one too many local whiskies, as he climbed over the stile to the road, he disappeared and I saw he was lying face down in the mud. I offered him a lift which he accepted, both of us were silent on the short drive home and I left him at the bottom of the drive to where I was staying. Imagine my surprise the next morning when he came down to breakfast dressed in a police uniform OOPS. After the words from the visiting spirit, I had a very restless night and the next day I packed my bags and headed back home, not at all sure what my destiny was, and more than a bit put out to be leaving Skye.

There have been many more visits back there and on a recent one with Roger, we stayed at a hotel close to Culloden Moor on the way, which is the site of a terrible battle in 1746. I was awoken by the noise and wondered what the heck was going on? Then saw troops marching straight through the bedroom, I tried to get their attention and ask them to go somewhere else, this proved difficult as they were in full battle mode and ignored me or didn't hear me. So I decided to pull the blankets over my head and try to get some sleep. I heard the battle all night and got annoyed that Roger was sleeping soundly oblivious to the soldiers apparently marching through the bedroom making a hell of a noise.

On another holiday in USA, it was really hot and we were cooling of in the swimming pool, there were a couple with their son who was about 8 years old, we spoke to each other and they said to the boy, hey these folks are from England, he came over and said that he lived in London and kept asking his parents when he was going home? His parents apologised and said he really thought he lived in England and that he could speak in many British dialects even though he had no contact with anyone from there. To this he started speaking cockney, followed by a very aristocratic accent, telling us about the latest Sherlock Holmes book that had just been written, and asked how dear old Queen Victoria was. With this his parents were obviously very embarrassed and make a hasty get away. I wondered if it was a past life that he was remembering.

Another time in Denver USA we visited the museum, after joining a long queue we eventually made it to the admission desk, just then one of the museum staff asked if we were from England? We said yes, she asked if we had heard the radio broadcast the night before about crop circles. No we said we hadn't. She told us that a new crop circle had appeared that week in Wiltshire in UK, it was far more intricate than usual and appeared to be 4D, she said that people who" saw" spirit had reported seeing star people walking in and out of the 4D shapes inside the crop circle. We had a long chat about UFO's, crop circles and speaking to the spirit world. I asked if she wanted our email address to keep in touch. She replied No, we just had to make contact, everything is done now. I have no idea what that was about!

I was sat having a cup of tea idly watching the sea rush past on one of my cruises when a lady asked me if she could sit with me, as there were no empty tables. Of course I said, she sat down and began to read her book. She put the book down and we started to talk about the places we had visited, eventually we got round to beliefs and religion. She had been a nurse all of her life and was retiring. I became aware of a lady from the spirit world who came close and said, say to her Margaret, so I asked if she knew Margaret. She replied that she was Margaret, then I had stereo in both ears as she and the spirit stood next to me said that she was named after her Grand Mother. I realised that this was the Grandmother stood beside me. I was able to pass on many messages that she needed to hear. I think the main reason for the message was to help the lady's granddaughter, the grand-daughter is question was what we call an Indigo or crystal child and needed help. Too many of these gifted children are lost in the educational system long before they become old enough to make a difference and help the earth through the ascension. We talked about many things and the lady told me that her granddaughter found it hard to fit in with the family, who thought it odd that she saw and heard people from the spirit world and that no one else seemed to be able to see or hear them. I told 'Margaret' that I had also had these things happen as a child and that I was OK and now completely happy with speaking to dead people. We both had to laugh at the conversation we were having, two strangers who had just met talking about such things.

I never like to be home for my birthday and have had many adventures travelling around the world to celebrate. On one birthday we rode camels into the Sahara desert at sun set, just as the light was fading we stopped and allowed the camels to sit while we leant against them. I saw a black stallion galloping towards us ridden by a young man in a robe, as he approached he reached down and pulled me onto the horse with him and we galloped off, we didn't go very far before he bought me back to Roger, I think he must have realised I would be high maintenance and made a quick getaway.

Another time in Mexico a Mariachi band, serenaded me. All very nice until they decided to throw me into the swimming pool fully dressed! On the same holiday we had made friends with a family who were on holiday with their two teenage sons, the youngest was 15, after the incident with the band, later on that night, he knocked on our door, smiling, he produced a homemade bong he had made from an empty water bottle, and complete with a chunk of hash he had bought on the beach. Happy birthday he said, go on, light it up, we can share it. I told him that maybe we would light it tomorrow, as it was rather late . . .

Other birthdays have included, paragliding, riding on a dolphin (with her permission of course) going inside the pyramids, crawling around in a cave under a mountain just after an earthquake, climbing a 600 foot vertical waterfall in Jamaica and having wild sex on an ancient burial mound in Wilshire UK

Once on a trip back from Florida with my son, we sat next to a rock band that were travelling from USA to UK, I only had a carry on case and it was stowed in the overhead locker next to one of the bands case. They were extremely lively and loud all the way home and we joked that we wished we had taken whatever they had taken as they were in such good spirits. A few weeks later I was travelling to Iceland with the same case, imagine how embarrassing it was to have my case prove positive for traces of heroin! After a search of the case and a hand swab, I was told I could continue and thought back to the Florida journey.

Quite a few years ago, I had a lodger who had a cannabis plant hidden behind my rabbit hutch, one day while upstairs I saw this strange plant and when I found out what it was, told the lodger it had to go, he said just give it a few days as its nearly ready to bud. A short while later, the whole plant was cut down and the leaves were put top dry between newspapers. Haley one of my German Shepherds found it and started to eat it, as I pulled it out of her mouth she pulled back, determined not to give up her herb. Although she hadn't had much of it, she slept solidly for several hours. After that if she smelt anyone smoking pot, she followed the scent and tried to share their joint.

I have a friend who is a very good cook and loves baking cakes, while at her house once I noticed a large plate of cakes cooling on the kitchen table. While she was making the tea I thought I would eat one, after all she would probably offer me one with my cup of tea. She didn't. When I got home I felt quite strange and kept staring into the fire at the weird shapes and colours. After a while it got worse and I went to look in the mirror, not sure what I was looking for. All looked normal but I felt far from normal. I went to lie on the bed for a while and must have gone to sleep. I had a new witchcraft course starting that night and was woken by the phone ringing; it was my friend who asked if I had eaten one of her cakes? Yes, I said, I didn't think you would mind. No she didn't mind but wondered how I was as they were space cake laced with cannabis . . . . The first night of the course went well even though I admitted to the group I was accidentally stoned.

One night while in Jamaica, I was standing waiting to cross the road when a long limousine with black windows came to a stop right by me, the window came down and the driver called me over, I could see that he had a young lady sat next to him, he pointed to my pentagram necklace and said, "what's that", I told him I was a witch and what it represented, I showed him my silver pentagram ring, he grabbed my hand and pulled it into the car for a better look, I must admit I was a bit scared by now, so to ease the situation, I asked if the lady sat next to him was his girlfriend? He just stared and said no, she works for me. I asked what he did in Jamaica and he smiled and said I am a juggler . . . . A few nights later my friend and I decided to make a visit to the local cemetery and take a can of beer for a local man, who had recently died as a farewell gesture, we were going to pour it on to his grave. My friend and I soon became aware that we were not really wanted in that area and were being followed by several men, and being taunted by men on motorbikes. As if from nowhere, the large limousine appeared. The man again stopped and I said, hello, we meet again, after a few minutes; he wound up the window and drove away. The men following us asked, "Do you know him"? Yes I said, their attitude changed completely and they all wanted to be friends and buy us a beer. We continued to the friend's grave, shared a beer with him, and saw that someone had tethered two goats on his grave. Later that night when we saw the dead man's wife, we asked, did your husband like goats. No she said he hated them, he used to throw stones at them. Oh dear I said, there are two tethered on his grave!

Arriving back at the hotel, the cleaner was working on our room, she asked our names, I told her I was Lyn, and she said she was also called Lynne. Had I got any clothes I could give her please? I gave her a pair of beach shoes and she was pleased. The next night she arrived with "a gift" for us, it was a huge piece of cannabis; we thanked her and giggled about it, joking where we could hide it as we didn't want it. My friend decided to hide it in a box of tampons as no one would look there. It sat there for several days and one day after a few rums, my friend said she was going to roll a joint and use some of it. She only had two puffs of it and turned from pink to purple to green in seconds. Then she rushed to the bathroom and was sick, after a while lying on the bed she got up and said everything was red and green, she said she could see straight through the wall but on trying to walk through it realised it was solid. Then she bent over and screamed as she said she could see right through her body. This went on for a while and then she started being sick again. The sickness lasted all night; she was lying on the tile floor in the bathroom covered by a sheet. The next day she was back to normal but felt terrible. The "stuff" went in the first bin we found.

Another day we were sat by the pool having a beer and enjoying the sunshine, we had heard about a local dance called the butterfly dance. We asked the bartender if he would show us the dance. He shook his head and replied, no I can't, I have to be "aroused" so my friend decided to whisper naughty words in his ear, soon he said he was ready, so standing up straight, use your imagination here, a certain part of his anatomy was the body of the butterfly, as he danced about his arms became the wings of the butterfly, we were laughing so much we didn't see the boss approaching, the bartender had though, he dived down behind the bar and when asked what he was doing, he said counting the glasses, don't be ridiculous, he said, I want to speak to you, stand up, luckily as he stood up, everything had gone back to normal . . . .

Arizona and TX 2012 This bears too close!

Beautiful Isle of Skye

building our house

DEVILS TOWER KNOWN FOR CLOSE
ENCOUNTERS OF 3RD KIND

FLORIDA 2010 Brrrrr Helping a sick aligator

Glastonbury Tor

LYNS GUIDES GRAVE

Meeting the Kangaroo's in Australia

Sacred Silbury hill Wiltshire

Standing stones at Avebury

Thailand 2013 Meeting a Python

Chapter Seven

More people seem interested in spiritual development

Everywhere seemed to be flooded with an interest in all things spiritual, lots of TV programmes, new spiritual magazines, celebrity mediums, different types of healing, it seemed we were being bombarded with spiritual development. This had a knock on effect on the number of people wanting to join circle, so now I was running five circles a week, along with readings, and Reiki share nights, it was a busy time.

After 2000 of course we would have 2001, so it would start with 01.01.01, this was predicted to bring a huge surge of spiritual enlightenment to earth, these special dates followed on for the decade and became known as powerful days and when portals would be opening up in different parts of the world. 02.02.02 bought even more energies and of course time seemed to speed up even more. As we progressed through the decade, we had 03.03.03, 04.04.04, 05.05.05, each bringing their own changes and energies. Another strange thing was happening as well, people were seeing these number configurations everywhere from car number plates to waking up during the night to see the clock showing 2.22 or 1.11, 3.33, 4.44 etc. It was interesting to hear the discussions at circle as we all compared our experiences and thoughts on why we were seeing these numbers. We passed the year 06.06.06 and 07.07.07 and were told that 08.08.08 marked the opening of a portal called the Lions gateway; this would bring visitors from other worlds closer to ours. More and more amazing pictures of UFO's were printed and remarkable accounts of sightings from ordinary people who had seen these crafts. Some were seen over nuclear plants and some over air bases. I was re assured by my guides of what they had said all those years ago about the world not being allowed to destroy the earth with nuclear weapons.

Finally we reached 09.09.09 and then arrived at 2010, only two years to go now till the Magical 2012! There is a very interesting book called Angel numbers which has an in-depth explanation of what the meanings of these repetitive numbers may mean to the individual.

I was interested in the teachings of a person known as Little Grandmother; she gives talks and workshops all over the world. A friend asked if I would go with her to one of these workshops to which I readily agreed. A short while later I had a phone call to say she had found us two places at one of Little Grand Mothers workshops, but the difficulty was it was in Santa Fé New Mexico. We thought about it for five minutes and decided to book the plane tickets. It was a long journey changing planes at Chicago and on to Albuquerque, then a shuttle bus to Santa Fé. We were not ready for the cold weather, it being minus 21 degrees when we arrived. The workshop was really good and there were people from all over the world who had travelled just as we had. Little Grandmother called us the tribe of many colours and said many times that the light workers on Earth right now were the brightest of the bright, the strongest of the strong, and that we didn't need teachers to tell us what to do, as we were the people we had been waiting for. She went on to say each person working for the light and to help bring in the energy of the new age had agreed to be here before their birth. Although many were finding it hard here on earth, she repeated that we were the strongest of the strong and could and would cope.

The workshop ended in us chanting and meditating together, Little Grandmother then went into a light trance and over shadowed by her spirit guides and helpers gave us all messages to help us with our future work. A few months later Little Grandmother came to UK but it was far more of an adventure to travel to New Mexico to see her.

Chapter Eight
Wilma and Little Socks

Wilma is a good friend who is also a member of circle, she is a trance medium. This means she goes into an altered state of awareness and allows one of her guides to speak through her, it's not at all scary, her guide has a very good sense of humour and we have had some excellent evenings with spirit through Wilma's work. We can then ask questions directly to spirit through her and get answers directly from spirit through her guide; these can be personal questions or universal questions. Wilma has agreed to allow me to share a few of the questions and answers here with you now to which I am greatly honoured to do. The following are some of the questions commonly asked and answered by Little Socks.

To begin any conversation with Little Socks, he would want you to understand that he works within a group of souls as spokesperson. He has been elected as spokesperson, as he has lived upon the Earth several times. I am aware of 2: once as a Saamari on the African plains, and the other as his life, from which he works with me in trance, as that of a Kiowa American Native, who knew life before and during the White man's coming. They named him Little Socks due to his moccasin style footwear. He has never revealed his true native name. He is able to confer with this group of souls, and to lift away from me to confer with the audience's spiritual groups for any pertinent information required, though more often than not he has a clear understanding of how the group will proceed beforehand and weaves the answers into his replies before they are asked. He is amusing, encouraging, loving and quick to put forward his philosophy, frequently taking up where he has left off with individuals and their understandings. It is his sincere desire to no longer be required, to become redundant, as all will be able to reach their own guides and their higher perspective themselves. So it is from his favourite "box of soap" that I will begin.

I will be using his words throughout, dating the transmissions. The content is by no means fully representative of the philosophy delivered over the years, as I have dipped randomly in and out from the rather large cookie jar to give an idea of his works on set topics Lyn wished to be included. I hope to produce a larger publication one day, if interest is there. I have always worked from audience request rather than pushing the universe. I wish also to thank all who have supported me and have given their "ears of listening" to Little Socks, in whatever part they have played!

I shall also insert, as footnote references, 2 messages given to me before Little Socks had begun speaking openly to groups to show the constancy of his messages. It may help some when reading to allow a setting aside of, does this fit with what I know, to allow more of an approach of, what if this was so. Take nothing that does not fit with what rings true in your hearts. I do not wish to create cognitive dissonance within any of you. This is simply another perspective.

(27-1-14)

We shall begin with what we come here to teach all, and to reiterate for those who have heard us before, to remind you that it is your birth right to be here upon this planet to have spirit guides with you at your sides at all times. Now because that is a birth right, and all of you have this, does not mean all of you use this. So therefore you all are on your way of using this, which we are very proud and happy for. That is how I wish to begin is to congratulate you all, for you are on your road of remembering how to be human upon this earth plane.

Now also along with that, it is for us to remind you, to encourage you to place highest and best to all that you do, be it upon your spiritual contact or be it upon your baser materialistic life. Placing highest and best on *all* that you do places that of the light of that best there, which your spirit guides, can then pick up the strands of, and formulate the path through for you. So therefore it becomes an easy thing for you to do: once you have this connection with your spirit, once you have placed your highest and best, to walk thereon this path, and to know that it is just this, as *perfection for you at this time*.

Now this then leads on for us to remind you that this now, that you are within, is being created by you within your mind sets and beliefs at each moment of time, which then leads us to remind you all that time is actually an illusion. It is all now, but you are within the material earth plane, so therefore you are affected by the appearance of it. But by reminding you that you are creating: that which is here in material form, that which you are learning, and that which confronts you . . . well comes across as lessons for you and your group as human beings upon this planet now. They are brought to you by spirit. This is one of their main tasks is to co-create with you that which is required for you.

Now this would lead me to remind you that you are forever learning. This does not stop. You are forever changing. This does not stop.

We shall then move on to remind you all, as you go along placing this highest and best, and communicating with your guides as you walk upon it, and having trust – ah that is the magical thing. It is the most difficult thing to do to trust that you are actually there on this perfect highest and best path for you, to then remind you to be constantly lifting therefore from your fear base.

You live within an earth plane that is of relativity. You understand this. It's made of this and of not-this. So therefore it is your choice, as you walk this earthly path, to be choosing between the "this" and the "not-this". It is there for lessons. It is there so that you are slowed, so that you have more learning capability. Now of course this ah . . . no they say for me not to mention that here. We will mention that later. For you to walk along and to forever to be lifting yourself, do not be expecting never to have "not-this" in your life: a less than what you would wish to be, a less than perhaps a loving being, for it is part of your makeup of being a human being, and you will not be cutting it off as if a leg gangrenous from your body. You instead learn to lift it to the light, to honour and respect it, for it is its own . . . um let us say creation in itself, for it to be allowed to be within a plane of existence in which it can be, but for you to choose not to be there with it.

Those are the main points we would wish to remind you of. Well you say: well I never knew it in the first place, and we are saying: yes you do. You have forgotten, and to stress that we are all very proud of you.

Fear Base
(17-1-07)

Now you think: ah, of course we all have our fears. Of course we all have certain things that hold us back from being our true selves. This is what I am speaking of 'temerity'. Not being bold enough to be the you that you are truly are, walking upon this earth as it is today, for it is most difficult for you, especially for you who are of the light, more attuned to the light, more attuned to being the human being of which is meant to be walking this earth, for you to walk proudly and strongly without um 'setbacks' let us say, both within your outer world and within your inner mind.

You may think it an odd topic for me to bring to you, but I think the truth of it touches all of you to some degree. Some of you are much stronger than others in the feel of your path and the trust in your guides and the link that you have with them, but still you have your doubts and your worries, your concerns. It is part of being upon this earthly plane, and that is why you go to your spirit source, we would hope, to/for counsel.

But then you will come back at times and say: Ach well was that me, or was that my true guidance? And so you go to another of your friends and discuss to seek counsel from them. You go to your groups. You go to your church meetings. You seek out others who are gifted in this way with speaking to those in spirit for your guidance, when in truth in your heart you know that what your path *can* be is for you to desire and to choose and to walk it strongly and firmly with great trust. This is difficult in your world is it not? (Yes) So you walk with unsteady feet at times. They are stronger, and at times they wobble, and you feel that you are falling or have fallen—temerity.

You shake in your boots. You feel that the ground is shaking when in truth it is you in your boots that are shaking the ground. The ground is quite firm underneath your feet. Your guides have assured you of this, for as you set your desires, you of these abilities let us say, of this stage of your development let us say, all have the ability. Even the younger one here who feels that she is stepping within those who are more able, she is just as able to set her feet—all of you—your feet upon your path, with a firmness and a trust that your guides are with you and are helping you, and it is-as-it-can-be set to the highest and best.

I have gone on and on about this before. You have heard me many a time before and again I will bring it back to you, to remind you that this is one of the largest lessons and the most difficult for you upon this earth plane for you to truly walk, truly walk. Not to wear it as a coat. Not to give it lip service, but to truly live it, here upon this earth **now** as reality, to be living life as best as it can be. As best, as highest and best, you have set it there. It is as it is. To not look at it in any different aspect, for you have placed it there, and your guides have helped set you there upon your path. They have lit the path. The foot prints have already been there cast, for you are casting a fishing line to your future of which you have already trodden, and you are only merely following yourself to this brighter future in which you are already existing within. You are understanding multi-dimensionalities? This is where I am going now.

So your futures, you are asking them to pull you forward by your request, by your desire. This is why you can have any desire for anything within you, for all the multi-dimensionalities of all realities of which you can be are there for you to be existing within, if not able within this life, then within other consciousness of other lives. It is free will. It is your choice.

Again it is worn as a jacket. You do not have true belief and faith within it for you to walk truly this path, temerity yes. They are telling me to pause, to stop for a moment to ask if you wish to ask questions before I walk forward with this, if you so desire me to.

(You say we walked it before?) Yes (Can you explain that?) You have understood before in my conversations that all time is now? It is an impossible concept for you upon this earth plane, for you to fully grasp, to hold, for it is impossible for you truly to. But you have heard me go on about it yes?

So if all time is now and you are on the fulcrum, as this one here, I was pointing out to her: that the now, the fulcrum-of-now is your power point, and that all is radiating out from the now-of-which-you-are. All of what exists in future and pasts upon all existences is based and balanced upon this now, now. The now, it is all happening all at once. So therefore all that you have been and will be and can be and all-that-is is you. And you are also your unique self, as you are sitting here with us here. Large concepts yes.

So therefore when I stated that what you are doing is casting a line to capture a fish to be pulled along, as in a boat. You know the fish will pull upon the line with great strength, it is pulling you into that future of which you already have been existing within and exist now. Yes? (Yes) But you are not focused upon in this now, for you are your unique self within this now. Yes you understanding better now? (Yes) Any more questions before I proceed, if you so wish me to do so. I shall proceed then yes?

We wonder at times how to make you . . . that is not the right choice of words, to get you . . . that is not the right choice of words . . . for you to understand fully, to fully grasp, to fully grasp and hold on to, without letting it go again, this concept that we speak of, that you are truly creating that which is for you. Remembering of course the conversations of which we have had that of course you are sharing this reality, this relativity in which you exist, with many other souls, who are also creating their existences. And of course there will be lessons for many, and all are not meant for you.

But we set this aside, and we wish you to understand fully that to take this: more trust, less temerity, less shaking of your boots, this shaking of this ground, and to walk: more firmly, more proudly, *knowing* that your guidance is there with a light shining, holding it as a lantern for you to see the steps that should be taken, and to trust in your heart of hearts that that which feels right for you is exactly as you—it is.

Highest and best, always place it there. Remember my conversations of intent. Consider this deeply when you place that which you desire to this path of yours, for the intention then leads you to many lessons. Remember also that what is deep within your heart is your true intent, not that which you can voice with great sincerity. When deep within your heart you have a very different belief of that which you are and *can* be. So I am again encouraging you to 'clean house', you understand this expression, to keep sweeping the cobwebs. It is an endless task for the pesky spiders go weaving again to catch you up within their webs of fear, old fear-based.

So we are encouraging you to keep your house clean, to take time every day in the beginning of the day, in the middle of the day, as you proceed to clean and sweep to highest and best to place all that you are, all that exists within and without to highest and best, and to trust that it is that.

I wish you would walk this path. I wish you would taste its full power, for this is where you find your true peace of mind, for where has the fear gone? Where has the temerity gone? Do you not have peace of mind for you *know* that you are as best as you can be, and all is? So what is there to fear or to fret about?

You know that you have your guidance and you are as-one. So you walk ever connected, knowing that their knowledge, the higher perspective is ever at your 'finger tips' you say—Finger tips! Odd expression you have—finger tips! We would not use that expression—We are within you. We are within your breath. We are within the substance of you. We share that of which you, as you call your dimension. We share it with you. We are that close. We walk with you, within you, and this is what we ask of you: to bring us in so close that we become physically inseparable in—I do not mean inseparable. I mean indistinguishable.

So as you breathe, you breathe together, and as you walk, each step is taken together, for you are as-one. Do you understand that expression I bang on about so much? You are as-one. There is no separation. You reach for your guides and you feel that they are separate from you still, many of you. Many of you feel them much closer, but many of you still feel that they are a will-of-the-wisp on a pesky wind, of which you must catch hold of as it drifts by before it is gone again. We are not of that. We are the very breath of you, the wind of which you breathe. That is where we exist. And to have firmer knowledge of this, we feel that it would help you maybe to understand, to fully grasp and hold onto and not let go of this truth, that you walk without the temerity and true trust, faith, and become human beings once again upon the earth, the new family of man of which you are a part of the emergence. Who can again live upon the earth in joy and true peace within, as-one with their spirit, their higher self, their guidance—we in the spirit world, who are as-one with them in the love, of which existence all is made of.

So in truth what you are doing as you walk—Ah they say pause a moment and ask. I am moving on. This is a pause position. Any questions before I move on?

(If we have freewill, even having trodden the pathway already, can we change our pathway?) Of course you have freewill. You can do as you will, but as I stated within a mini statement that within this life you have only certain pathways, for you are born within this body, within this flesh, within these circumstances inured within this society, so you cannot go and live as a tree suddenly or as a sparkle of the stardust, for you are within this body. If you wish for that experience, then you can be, and have been, and are a part of this existence. Again you have struggled to grasp the conception that you are everything and your unique self, both. You are all. Someone at some point recently asked me about Archangels and felt that they had never lived upon the earth. Well how can everything be as-one and not have touched all-that-is, especially such a high being as this that is evolved?

So I am saying to you: yes you have complete freewill, and that you can change your course at any time, although it takes time, for you live within your time-based relativity! And of course we have slowed it so that you do not make such a mess of it. I nearly swore there, oh dear! I should not be doing that. Yes? (Yes thanks) This is why it is slowed. This is why it is quickening. We have discussed this. You understand these concepts, yes good. Any more question before I can move on, if you wish me to? I shall move on then yes.

I began, again with my movement forward with speaking to you here that all is one. Well we have stated that. What I was saying to you that as you continue your pathway, oh dear . . . It is as you gather more and more of your consciousness together in balls of lives, of experiences within one life, within many lives, within all of the lives you become a greater and greater ball. Just as your planets become planets. They gather bits of dust and consciousness to them do them not, material which binds within their gravity.

The now-fulcrum, of which you are in the existence of *now*, has an effect upon all that is. This is what I am saying in this. And it is very important for you to understand therefore the meaning of the importance and the responsibility it has upon you, and what you are doing within your walking upon this earth: within your temerity, within your faith and trust, in your joy and your peace of the true walk.

If we could raise this vibration to resonate upon this frequency of true trust, the earth would oh be such a different place. You know this, but you also know of the relativity of which will continue to exist upon her planes. So I am saying to you that eventually you will

not wish to require this relativity as you progress, and
to move on to that which—I am not saying that you all
are about to die and move on, no, no. I am saying in time
there will be other dimensions for you to exist within, not
only upon this earth of which you exist anyway, for you
exist as all things anyway. Ah you understand me? Ah I
am not getting my point across . . . .

You know as you walk, you gain experience? What
does experience give you? It gives you growth. What
does growth give you? It gives you a consciousness. It
gives you a desire, a yearning, a yearning for change, for
progression, for things never to remain the same. They
will not, so never expect them to be. So many living
on the earth expect all things to remain unchanged.
The earth is altering. The earth is changing and her
temperatures and her water levels. Well of course she is.
She is a living, existing being and she will be changing
just as you are, and everyone panics so. How dare she
have an existence and not stay stable for us, when we do
not stay stable, and we are not remaining stable in what
we are doing within her realm.

I am not side tracking. What I am trying to explain again
is the power point of your fulcrum and the importance
of it, and also too that you are amassing growth. That
you are amassing consciousness, that you are amassing
this ball of you, of which is growing and growing and
continuing to, as 'rungs of a ladder' let us say, lift into
this being of a human, of a human being walking truly.

Again we come back to this. I come back to this to say: then you become a master, and a true master and teacher of this life on this earth. And then this is collecting for the masteries of all the lives. The fulcrum touches all of those lives of which you are, and therefore touches all of existence.

(One of things we find difficult at the moment with the time being quicker, things happen quicker as whenever you have a thought it happens and takes a bit of getting used to) You understand how it is like within the spirit world? (You think and it is) You are a part of spirit. You are becoming as-one with your spirit guides and you expect your life not to alter and to become more like spirit? (Yes but it's been the same for such a long time, difficult to separate the spirit thoughts from the psychic ones) You do not any longer. It becomes one. You're understanding me? (I do, but we think something and then it's there) That is how it is meant to be. You have only been given this great time laps within only this relativity-based dimension for you to learn the importance, for you to re-learn how to be human, to re-learn the responsibility to set all to highest and best. You have come here to remember, to operate within a very unusual field of existence, for you to operate to experience what happens.

Of you others find it difficult. Yes really hard) this is why we say it is not an easy walk to walk, but it is truly where your hearts have asked to go. (Yes) We have responded.

(Thanks, ask for it and when we have it we don't want it!) This is the temerity that I begin with. Yes it is, indeed it is, and it is your lack of faith and trust that it is just fine. (OK) It is as it is meant to be. It is how human beings are meant to walk upon the earth. They have walked before upon the earth as this, and you have forgotten. You wish it back so much in your lives. You ask and ask for it, and when it is gifted, put there upon

The platter: oh it gives me indigestion! –Laughter— Too much chocolate, too sweet, too much sweet life! But it is truly how the human being is meant to be. So can you understand how far astray it has gone, and has been *allowed* to go, and why has it been allowed to go so far? For your freewill, for your lessons, it is the base of the earthly set up. (Thanks) Pleasure. Shall I continue? (Yes thanks)

Now you are seeing this golden light of the new dawn, proudly walking now, strong and tall, taking that which is the stick of you from the fire, the spiritual fire that is here and holding it high as a beacon for others to follow, saying: yes it is fine. We can do this. This is how it is meant to be. Be brave. Follow our footsteps as we are following from our future, you follow ours. We will all help each other, and pick each other up.

As you go to your guides for guidance, and you go to your circles, to your friends, you can be that for others. We

are asking you to continue, but we still remind you that
this golden future will not be all shinning shimmering
gold, for you still will be within relativity. Ah that is
what makes it such a challenge. This is why you have
chosen it. 'Easy-peasy' to walk like this when all is thus,
but when you have the opposite: who are there, who are
causing you great problems, who you feel are causing the
earth great problems herself, and who are causing great
problems not just to you, but your animal life—ah yes I
know—to all of which you hold dear. How dare they and
you—oh dear there you have slipped. You understand?

So you have chosen a very, I do not know the word—
'tricky', um growth enhancing dimension in which
to exist, especially in this time of great change. You
remember that you have chosen it, and remember that
you have chosen it well because you are able. Remember
that you have chosen it for you are the leaders, that you
are the beacon bearers, that you are the teachers, the
healers. You are the true leaders, and that has *nothing* to
do with your governments. The true leadership of this
world will become from those such as us here. I say 'us
here' because I include your spirit. Remember you are
here as your spirit, and you as-one.

I am not saying the walk shall be easy, but in truth it is as
easy as you allow it to be, because again I go back to that
point of temerity: to leave it behind, to walk in faith, that
it is as it is because you have placed it there the highest
and best, and can nothing be . . . it cannot be lived in any

other way, *no matter what it appears to you* here within, caught within this relativity—big challenge yes.

It is one of the most important lessons that we ask you to do. It is one of the highest lessons that we ask you to do. And we are not saying that you are failing miserably. We have come with encouragement, with love, with healing, with higher perspective, and wish you to hold that torch even higher and to know that light is the beacon not only of your love, but of our light of our love, and it shall never go out for we are ever with you.

And we go back to that point once again, but we repeat these things for you truly—you believe it one moment and it slips from your hands—temerity. We wish that for just an hour—sometimes you will achieve it. Sometimes for half a day some of you, or a day, or several days, and it slips again. Of course it will. We are not asking you to be 'perfect'! What a silly concept! We are asking you to pick yourself back up and to remind yourself again to rise above from that fear-base, to rise again to your spirit source, to that love and to walk forward again, to pick up that torch once again that is laying on the path lighting the footstep just one in front of you and take them one at the time. Trust that they will take you where you wish to go, for that is the only place where it can lead, for you place it there.

Again we are going around in circles with my information for you, but this is the message we have come. This is the main message that they wish me to deliver to somehow give you the strength to walk daily all day, all through your nights, at every moment of your life and be a true master. I would say that there are none upon the earth truly today. So do not beat yourself up for being human, but strive to be a true human being and allow yourself that gift of the peace and the joy that is your birth right.

It almost does not feel right when the world seems so wrong, for you to wake and be filled with the love and the joy of that of life. You look at your papers.

You turn on your news. You talk to your fellow man, and you wish to take to your bed again and try to awaken again with: this spirit, this feeling of this rightness, this joy, this peace, this closeness, this great love, not only for yourself, but for all-that-is as it shines as brightly as it can be. Remember that all those who are amongst you within all of their 'relativity' let us say, 'dimensions' let us say, 'levels of learning' let us say, oh how else can we put it . . . and whatever their free-choice has directed them to walk *their* footsteps, that it is *their* free-choice, and it has really nothing to do with your and yours.

I am not asking you to cut out your heart and have no compassion! Quite the opposite, I am asking you to grow your compassion and allow your heart to enlarge, to encompass and to hold *all*-that-is, as you have been and are, and see it all as-one as you are, and all as unique as you are—both and separate, you understand. So you are all-and-everything and you are your unique self, as all is.

Path
(1-6-05)

So here you are, you are born, and you have chosen for the experience the focus of a certain um 'bowl of soup', for lack of whatever to say! And so you come into life and you cannot find the bowl, never mind the soup. And you say: Where is my path! It is not at my feet, yes? (Yes)—Laughter—So you stumble upon, yes you think you find a bowl, and it is not the right soup, and: no, that is not right. You know you have a story with bears. No, yes, ah never mind.

I am trying to say to you that you are creating your life as you go along. (OK) You have come with a desire for experience. You then come into life living, for that bowl of soup to be searching, but first of all, because of the veil, you need to unravel what that bowl of soup might be. And I say to you: yes it can be of many flavours, yes and it can be of many temperatures, as within the bear's story for children. Ah it could even be in a cup!

But the experience is of soup. So it is not so 'hard wired'. You can gain experiences within many scenarios. It is not as if you must meet a certain lady called Grace, and have 5 children. You understand with a black dog and a red car. No it does not work in this manner, although there are certain things that are 'hard wired' within your life for the experience, for these can be of benefit for others. You understand why they are there in this way.

(Is that hard wired permanently?) Ah yes as designed before you were born, to be in the tapestry of the picture, let us say, (OK) although many of the details are missing, and you place them there through choice.

You understand what the bowl of soup is about though, do you not? (I do) Yes, yes. I'm just hankering to climb upon my soapbox, you see and speak of the reason mankind is upon the earth. And that, you understand of your connection with spirit as being your birth right, of your rising above your fears, (Yes) to walk proudly, as human once more upon the earth, of which most here have sadly turned their back to. (Yes) Yes, hence end-eth the lesson. (Thank you) People get so hung up on this soup bowl idea, you see. You cannot be off your path ever. All experience is of validity.

(8-8-12)

I want to remind you all that it is not us that choose your pathway for you. It is you that chooses it. It is you that have chosen it before you have come into this body, into this earthly life. You know this, yes? And it is also your guides that work with you as to your desires. Now not all, of that pathway is set in stone, and to achieve an objective there are often many paths that one can surmount, travel upon.

So therefore, when we are presented with a question of this: is this the right path for me, we turn that back and say: well, all of life is pathway. You cannot really ever be off of it, for all that you encounter within your life is set there from that which you create from your mind sets, your belief, your intent.

So therefore you cannot be off of it, for this is how your world is created. It is made up thus. So therefore it is always you that is the creator of it. So therefore we would say to you, if your heart is in it and you are happy within it, and it is bringing you learning and experience, then it certainly is a good path, a path for you to be upon.

(2-7-12)

Some people believe that they have to be walking on a path. To be happy they must find their path. And they feel that their path, I have said this before, others may have heard me, but they find, they decide that this path must be like a tightrope. A very thin line, very easy to fall off and very difficult to find, and also they must be told, like from spirit: that's the rope. Never mind that it goes over the canyon, you know: you walk it dear! This is not so. Again you are forgetting that it is your choice. That experience—we use the expression that it is all valid: that your path is everywhere around you, that anywhere that you could put your foot is your path. It is not so restricted.

What you are seeking is a quieter mind and an open heart to then fill with the love and the light. That is pure freedom, for you let go of looking for yourself, for it becomes unimportant, for you are working for the higher, the highest and best for all, and realise that you who-you-are is loved and important for you, yes that individual, I am not saying that you are not, but it becomes less important than the greater that you have found with the link from your heart to us.

It would help in a way if you learned the process of healing, for this will help you to attach more easily to allowing the "light of source", they say you use these words, to come through you, and to help to link and to help you to let go of what you are holding onto as mind, and to link and let go, to go further into spirit, that attachment, you understand me, and to allow it to flow. Choice—part of that is your link to spirit. Yes that also gives you this.

What you are finding unsatisfactory of seeking "you" in the mind is that you are missing the most important lesson that you are more than the "you-in-the-mind". You are part of source and part of connection with spirit, your higher self and all the other lives that you are living at the same time. You are part of it all, and you are trying to limit "who am I" in trying to find "who am I", when you are so much more. So no wonder you are not happy within trying to limit it within, yes? Learn to open and connect. Choice, but ask for your protection and you know all the drill there, yes. Enjoy the journey.

Protection

(26-06-06) (LS Good evening) Good evening (Um, There's theory coming from some places that we do not need to put protection around us to help keep us safe. Is it necessary for us to have protection around us at all times?) You know dear one your thinking, and your growth of thought, and being of experience continues onwards. You begin with the feeling of the fear: working above the fear-base, lifting yourself above it, connecting to your guidance, feelings at every step. You lighten yourself, do you not? And as you go further with this, and have spirit guidance with you at all steps of your stepping, as you press it to highest and best, you are so walking. You are therefore so lifted above your fear-base and so full of light that no you do not any more need to be fearful, for you have lifted above it! Does that answer you? (Yes thanks) Ah ha so indeed, you have the feeling you need to protect, then protect. Ask for the protection. It is always there for you. It is only the fear-base, which will magnetise the need for protection. And indeed another way is to step above and to fill yourself with light. Yes, our pleasure. (Thanks) Pleasure.

(9-12-12)

I think that all of you will find that as you journey
and give all of yourself more love and light that your
compassion for others will never end. Your love will
never stop. You will become stronger in your love of self
to walk forward in that strength. And in the unity with
the higher perspective of spirit, rather than speaking and
listening to your lower selves of your minds, you will gain
the structure; we wish to say higher perspective, from
spirit to help you to cope. Things will get easier. It will. It
is not-oh dear, at times it feels almost it is a quagmire. You
will never escape. You are being pulled down from the
woes of: this one needs help and this one is in trouble and
this one and this one and I don't know how to. We wish
you to be out of that, yes but you are asking for advice in
how to cope while in that quagmire.

Well we have already asked you to fill yourself more of
light, to speak with your guides, to be more with their
higher perspective, for they are there. That is what they
are meant to be this birth right, and it is what they are
for, to work with you yes. You know that. I think it is
just practice and more practice at loving but not giving
yourself away—without giving yourself of power away,
you remain powerful within your love.

You all know about cloaks of colour, protection, you
use these words. You can utilise these. Yes they are
good practice as you say. It is good to ask yourself for

protection, to *know* that you are protected. This is what also you are asking

about in a way, but we also are trying to suggest for you to think about a time of being, in which the more full of light you are, you will not need that cloak of protection to cover the glimmer, for it shall shine so strongly. And that can only take practice from you, never mind the job. Never mind that this is really what you are here to do is to practice that. Lifting above, keeping within your centre of love, keeping it at all times, difficult yes. When you reach that stage, you definitely not be needing me, you will definitely not be needing advice, for you will be much better aligned as it were with your spirit

Lifting Above Your Fear Base/Good-Bad Dichotomy/ Judgement
(9-8-06)

(LS going back to what you said about lifting. I find it very difficult sometimes to feel content and happy. When walking under the trees, I suddenly think what is happening in the Middle East, and feel guilty as I should feel lifted for they are going through such tragic circumstances. I don't know how I should handle this.) In your own unique way, it is part of you to carry—I wish you to use the word 'compassion'. Um, 'guilt' is a very negative emotion, you understand this yes, and does not take you very far within lifted-ness. It would better behove you to use your lifted-ness to place the healing there for them, understanding that within your healing, in your placing it there for them that all-is-as-it-can-be, that you cannot see the larger picture, and it is as-it-can-be for the highest and best, and that is as it is.

It is difficult thing we ask you, for you cannot believe that the atrocities are for the highest and best, but you must take on board this knowledge that that which **you** perceive is illusion. It is set there for the lessons that have been *requested* by the humans upon the earth, and are there for a purpose of which you cannot perceive fully, for you cannot see the larger picture. You "cannot see beyond the end of your nose", I believe is the expression.

I am not asking you to be lifted and raise your nose, and not to cut off your compassion, but I would strongly suggest that you do not feel the guilt that you are living a fine comfortable life, when there is such misery. Use the time, as I stated before, to see things all as perfection. It is, I agree, a difficult place to hold! This is why you have spirit with you. This is why you connect with your spirit guides within these times of your feeling as this for their help, for you to see within a different perspective, yes? (Yes) So that is the other part of my answer. Go to your guides. Always go to your guides. That is what they are there for: to help you within these times, and to help you within the times when you feel fearful, and also to help you in the times when you feel joyful and lifted, always at your side, within you, within your breath itself. It permeates you—the spirit. (Thanks) Now that shall do. They say that is enough. Will this be enough for you? (Yes) Pleasure.

. . . You do not choose upon your birth a role of the 'bad guy' or the 'victim'. As I say it happens subconsciously at times through the life of having a choice of playing this role.

Therefore what I am saying is when you come upon this life, that not all is set within the tapestry. Certain events are stitched in, of which gives you the ability to learn that which you wish to practice more upon, but not all is there of definite. You have freedom of choice. You forget this.

(OK, just certain choices we have?) You have freedom of choice within all of it. (Right) Much of it is, as I stated unconscious as you go through your life, but you still have freedom of choice. Much is engrained within your mind sets, your understandings, your beliefs, of which many do not stand back and question and look at and upgrade. You understand, you know bring up to date.

So many of you continued with, I referred to rosy-coloured spectacles, of spectacles of different tints, and 'that is the world, and that is the world as it is'! Well you forget that everyone else has their own glasses on, and they see a very different world from you.

So yes indeed, your healing light is always of much greater strength than that of the reverse. And that is why we say so strongly that it is of such importance for more and more of you to become those beacons of the light, to strive to be lifted above, beyond this engagement of *your* mind within 'that is not right. That is bad.' Yes the relativity, your words of defining things, and to lift above and see again, as I state, that all is as-it-is, is as-it-can-be and is of perfection, for those who are on board have created it thus.

Now you know therefore through that answer, that the more of you who become beacons of light will then be shaping a new reality, and this is what your New Age is about. Do you understand where I am going? (Yes I do) So you understand how much power you humans have, and how you shun and will push it away from yourselves. And we are asking you to take it up as a banner! You are most powerful and creative, just as we are in spirit, but it is here in a different format of reality—of relativity for you to live in a slowed time structure let us say, for you to remember again, and to walk feeling detached. To remember again that you are all as-one, all of love. Therefore I am saying that the atrocities are not of un-love. It is all of love.

(So these atrocities are 'stitched in' as you would say?) Not all are stitched in no. Much is based upon the freewill. The freewill of those who choose, and feel that they have no choice, for their glasses say that: 'this is what the world is, of course it is and you're crazy!' Well they have not questioned. They have not meditated. They have not given themselves time to stop, for the listening to their guidance for the higher perspective, to even consider that all are unique and all are of one, and there is no difference. And therefore you are upon the earth given this bad/good, for you to work out once again that it is all of-one! That will suffice? (Yes thanks) Our pleasure, you are not still understanding how much it means. You consider it.

(9-8-06)

(I have a question about knowledge. I feel that we are all here to learn lessons. Old people gain so much knowledge and insight throughout their life and would like your reassurance that the things we learn go forward when we move on as it seems such a waste of knowledge otherwise to just-) First of all I would like to say that not all move forward. Many of your elderly are as fixed within their mind sets, beliefs, their spectacles of different shades, as they were when they were a child. (Right)

It takes great courage to question one's own reality. (It does) It takes great courage to consider that what one has been taught, and that what one leaves as a truth may be a stepping stone to something of a greater truth, of a different truth, which may throw all of your belief system into a scatters, as sticks falling from a tower, and then where will you be, You're frightened of this, for you are frightened of 'madness' you say.

Ah but you forget you see, that is why you have your spirit guides, and this is why we encourage all of you who are here, most important lesson is for you to be encouraging others in some way to be listening to their inner self, their . . . If they do not believe in guides then use words of which they can understand. (Some do but don't even realise) Indeed, so you can use their own belief systems and words.

I would say also too that you must remember that all experience is valid. So therefore, the life of that one, who has chosen to sit in his little rut in the road and to cover his head with his hands and not look up all of his life, has experienced this situation, and it will be part of what is. It is all parts of the play once again, and of choice. You would not think that anyone would choose this, but you would be . . . oh dear there are more these days, but so few do choose to lift even one eye. And this is part of the problems your world is experiencing, for each holds stoically as of river of to their bit of their bank side, and say 'this is reality', when they miss the river and all of the land that it involves, which is all of what man and existence is. [1] (Reference to "The River" 10-3-93)

---

[1] THE RIVER (10-3-93)
The first thing that is required is trust. Then life can flow as a river, with direction and power flowing to the source with constancy, allowing obstacles in its path to be

absorbed or left behind on the banks. To be thus means that Ego has no boundaries but as the bank that a part of that river wishes to examine as reality. Too many of you hold onto definitions of the bank as the totality of experience. This small segment can be idyllic or foul and pestonic. This trait is human in that living on Earth it is difficult to see the length(s) already traversed, for those which the Spirit knows as travelled in synchronicity. This forgetfulness is part of Earthly experience which is necessary to dramatize the scenarios of learning opportunities. Leaving the banksides to be flowing in constant apparent movement of realities (the banksides left to be what they are-which is conscious awareness) is feared by many who hold to defining self-descriptions of oft frequented banksides.

This severely limits the Is that is the Spirit self, for it stops the mind/consciousness from meeting new definitions of self and becoming aware of the diverse definitions which it limits it's being.

We repeat this message . . . for so many ignore its implications! Gifts are given and earned this is true but why believe in the Ego's definition of this life's potentials? Trust is misplaced. The Mind calls the shots and many decry the futility in not achieving the goals set by it, realising they have set themselves up to fail. This happens so Ego can prevail, for it is keen to keep consciousness within safe boundaries of "restful" banksides. Somewhere within each of you is knowledge of this scenario . . . It is like a willing for deep awareness, of remembrances and feelings of peacefulness never allowed by the fearsome egotist. Many nod and state understanding, whilst continuing to grasp to handholds that hold them fast to viewpoints currently comforting them . . . be they restful or plagued by "devilment".

We implore you to *LET GO*!! Let go of past definitions of self, remembering each passing minute creates this past. Go to Higher Self . . . that link to God, as it is called, then to that quiet space where nothing is materialised within forms of consciousness. THERE is freedom. This space is the building blocks of new awareness. THERE one can be in touch with the essences of creation, and create banksides with fluidity and grace which behoves the form of their creator—which is each of you. Only within the form of the river itself will you find the awareness that is space . . . which is essence without formed consciousness. The river then ceases to be hydrogen and oxygen molecules—Light in movement towards conscious form; but is redefined and the molecules become the banks, and then one flows within the true essence. Then one can pray and bring down consciousness in thought and form to re-shape oneself and the reality of one's banksides here and now!

. . . First be free of life patterns. Be ready for the new which rushes in like water bursting through a dam. Just resting can be a way for perceptions to take firm root. Let time soothe. Rest into us.

. . . Each soul has a rhythm which guides them through. This sound vibrates as sighs to dreams of memories held too dearly. Let go such sweet sorrows.

So when you are dying, you say 'passing over', finished of this earthly life, then all of your consciousness is then taken with you, and your experiences are not lost when you come to spirit. (Thanks) And they also help to shape. You are creating still that which you experience upon going to your spirit world. And it takes great time for them to come round to the idea that they have still a consciousness! Yes (Yeah) this will do. You understand now, (Thanks) pleasure, pleasure. Much is such vast in the answer, it is difficult to make small.

(20-7-05)

(How are we judged upon passing over?) I wish to make one statement to you that we do not judge you! It is only mankind who judges themselves. (Oh right OK) So I do not know how to answer your question, for there is no judgement. It does not exist.

(So those who have done bad things will be treated as equal as people that do good. Is that right?) **They shall**

find in their heart how to be with themselves. (Right)
Now in that statement, I chose my words with care, for
how you are with yourself involves more than just if
you have fine clothes and good food. How you are with
yourself—I shall climb upon my box and speak to you: of
being lifted without fear, of mind sets, beliefs, focus, you
know all of this. (Yeah) Of communication with us, of . . .
you know all of this!

So I ask you for one who does what you call 'bad things',
of which we have no knowledge of what truly bad things
would be, for this is part of your relativity in which you
exist only here. I would ask how one would accomplish
this, if one sat right with themselves? They would have
no need for judgement of self or others. It is this lack of
'being truly human' of this . . . well let me re-phrase this.
Being truly human is what you are here and here learning
to be. So therefore, it is part of being truly human to pass
through: your lessons, your stages, your levels as you call
them, your growth, you're learning. (Yes) And I am not
saying that a very learned one would not have still of a
judgement for self or others.

So you then must start 'weighing your grains from sand'
of the gold, and decide for yourself, of which you would
rather have collected upon your scale of 'good to bad'. Yes
you understanding me.

So therefore mankind has this conception that all is of
judgement upon passing over, and that if one has not
acquired the lessons, the stages, that one is expected of

one in that life, as 'all should be good', then they should have rap on knuckles and be sent for 'punishment life'. No, no this is karma . . . again your misconception. (Yeah, yeah) You understand where I am leading it. (Yeah)

I must say here here also, that there is coming upon this subject in your thoughts that, yes there are those who come here to do what is **perceived** to be 'bad',

for the growth of the 'good'. So can you qualify them as truly 'bad' when they have set themselves this task? So where is your judgement there?

So you must look and realise that those who are doing what **you** qualify as bad-to-your-good, which is upon— within your own world: mind sets, conceptions, beliefs, you understand your values, within **theirs** it is not of any problem at all. You have just not the knowledge of 'being in their shoes'. (That's right) So how can one judge the 'bad' from 'good'?

It is difficult upon the earth. We do not do it in spirit. It is not a good use of your energy. (No) There are times when yes, there is a time: for looking at oneself, for readjusting, for amending, for tuning up, so that one can: shine more brightly, be more lifted—oh off I go! You understand. But that is not judgement. That is a knowing one's self, and choosing again for the creating of oneself and one's life lived here. (Right)

Ah, so you wonder what this 'bad' chap does when he passes with: all of the killing, of the dead people, of the souls that he has dripping, and the heads banging at his belt. No, for you must understand that the tapestry has many threads, and **you** cannot see the entire picture by peering at one thread, of which you have the colour black attached to, of which black in your world is of 'badness'. You have no understanding of what this man has done, why he has done—yes of the bigger picture, and of the lessons for self and others.

What more can I say, except to encourage you, once again to release these judgment-thoughts? (Yes) That person, that chap, upon going to spirit will be the same as any other going to spirit. They will find themselves within the realm of their consciousness, of which they stepped from life, and from there they progress, as you do upon life. What is so different, although, in spirit they are re-connected more so with their higher perspective once again. (Yeah) I think I have answered this for you. (Yeah you have) I do not know how often I can encourage you to, implore you to release judgement. 'Put it in little bits in bin' you say.

(The reason I asked the question is because recently we had suicide bombers in London.) I am aware (I don't know if you followed that? You would have as you're in spirit, and was thinking really on the side of how they can be treated as equal as anyone else with what they done, but-) To many who do this step, it is of great—how often would you go to that length to uphold what you believe in? You understand me. There is qualities, of which are hidden, in much of what is done, as unable to be perceived by the other who does not exist within the shoes of the other. And you can say: They were 'coerced'. They were 'brainwashed'. (Oh yes) Then it is a great lesson for giving your power away, is it not! And think what a lesson this is, not only for that person who accomplished this deed upon the earth for him to grow in spirit from, but also for those upon the earth who look and discuss. And you do not realise that many come with this reason, to do this for this reason—to be that lesson.

You must also remember that you are more than just this one life. It is not like notches on—I do not know your expression. One life is of many. You cannot judge the consciousness of that being, from the one life in which they are living, fully, for it is only a spark of the great flame of their life! (Yeah OK)

(So you are saying that we have to learn all things that happen to someone to bring the soul to a whole. Is that right?) That is one way of conceiving that, of which we speak of your mastery, for you to achieve knowledge of that of ascendancy. And then—even then, you have choice of stepping from and into earthly shoes. But of all lives throughout, you—um it is difficult to explain rather large concepts, for your brains to cope with, when you are here in earthly. But if you know that all time is now, that all is one. Um think on this, then how can you be all-of-one? You are indeed all of all: that is being lived, and has been lived, and will be lived. (Yeah) Large concept. It is too large for you to hold, for you are such a small part existing and experiencing that-of-the-whole.

(So we need to love those people as much as those who have been killed?) They are indeed you. All is **you**. You treat them as yourself. And if you want to be harsh in judgement of yourself, then so shall ye be with others, and others shall be with you. And if you free yourself of this, then you shall live within a

world of 'free'—freedom to be-as-you-will. (Makes sense) There is your freedom. There is your unconditional love. (You explained it very well, great help, thanks) Pleasure.

(27-1-14)

(Why do certain bad actions take place?) Well I shall remain with my answer that certain actions take place for learning, not only for them, but for others. Certain actions, I will remain with my answer that certain actions take place because of mind sets and beliefs. They create the situation that this might occur.

Now you would think that if such thing was done—many of you hold a belief because you are used to time being linear past to future, rather than all time as now, as a fulcrum, and the pasts and the futures and everything happening all at once—you would consider that that person who had achieved, let us say a less than beneficial action upon another, upon mankind would then have to reap some process that would balance it in some way. That would make you feel there is as much light as there is not-light. This is not true, for it is all light.

So this man has, this woman has, this soul has achieved a less than loving act. Whatever is put out is what comes back. So it has magnetized the situation in which a not loving act can be produced. It has achieved bringing to it a non-loving actions, consciousness, energy let us say. It does not mean that in other lives it has to repent, do good or do service to make up for this, for it all is now. Hum it is hard for you to conceive. It is choice. And then you have the viewpoint of spirit that it is not written that cause and effect is a law, as you know it. It is simply that whatever you are, you create around you and magnetize. Yes, you bring to you. It is part of learning choice, of choosing to be higher and best for yourself and that other. Will that suffice?

(21:35)

(How do you view them?) Well you see we have a love of a light of unconditional love set upon all of those, but we do not condone or ascribe to their actions at that time. We understand that what they do is in line with their mind sets and beliefs at that time. They are therefore creating situations for themselves and for others to have lessons.

Now it will surprise you for me to say that in actuality in all of your "this and not-this", it is all made of love! It is all actually of the same clay, of the same substance. We recognise that from our viewpoint, for we see more than what this short play upon the earth is demonstrating of that consciousness, of that soul energy, for it is much more than this focus of this spot on this now of the floor, for it spans to all of the lives that it has lead, and will lead, and has lead.

Some that produce these atrocities, as you say, are sometimes, not always, very mastered folk who come upon this earth plane for this experience, of experiencing the antithesis you understand, the opposite. And also it is of a great service at times, surprisingly so. Not all. Most is simply mankind learning from mind sets and beliefs and behaving in certain ways that are less than helpful to others.

You must remember also that those, who are the victims often, more than often will have chosen that relationship for the chance for them to learn again of this. So that is how we view them.

(27-7-05)

(Can I ask one LS?) Ah yes. (I think you as the only person who could answer this. It goes back to the bombing a few weeks ago in London. What were their actual beliefs are about what they are doing? Where do they actually go after committing these atrocities?) You have an understanding of spirit life? (Yes)

You have an understanding 'where one goes when one departs here', yes? (Yes) This is the second part of your question.

It may surprise you that it is no different. There are those you feel that they are living a life that is not worthy, that it is not in line with serving the best that they would possibly share your space upon their demise! My sense of humour, excuse me.

In truth consciousness is consciousness. You're forgetting that all time is now, that you live all lives now. And that "that which is you" is more than just this spark upon the earth-plane. But for that spark upon the earth plane, where it goes, after you are no longer here upon this earth plane, it is no different. Your consciousness exists. It continues on.

Now we shall bring in the first part of your question, for explaining my attempt at the second! Ah I have spoken often of beliefs, of focus, mind sets. What man thinks and feels is what makes the man, I am saying to you. Now it would surprise you that those who have done this, it may be a show of their great strength of belief. Ah, would you be prepared to go so far within your beliefs, even within of goodness?

Now you must remember also I speak to you often of judgement—lack of. We do not judge. You do this for yourselves. So with lack of judgement, with experience of living life for the experience of that: which you belief in, that which you focus upon. All is free choice. It is **truly** free choice.

Therefore what we are saying to you: yes it does matter greatly in what I speak to you, and how you live your lives here: for remembering to be human, to lift above your fears, to communicate with spirit, all of these things. I am contradicting myself here in a way, for I am saying that experience is experience, and many come to this plane for the experience of that which is not of—um, I speak 'gutter snipes', yes I use this expression often—not of the highest attunement, for it is of **choice**. It would surprise you that some have come with a selected dedicated life, for that which is less than noble.

Why would one choose this, then you say. I say: it is for lessons for the others, and at times these people are of gifted/gifting for that . . . ah. How can you learn within a plane of relativity, if you have not the relative? 'This-that', 'not this-yes this', you understand, 'good-evil'. Someone must play the apart, mustn't they?

Now who, amongst all of you who upon this earth walk, are all masters in truth? For you are living all in 'now'; and in the 'all', that you are all-of-one, you are all mastered and of that source. So which shall draw the 'short straw'? Someone must play parts.

Consider a flower. The seed will blow in the wind. Some shall cast itself upon fertile soil in sun. Some will cast itself within barren—a crack in your pavement. This is not so unlike your human life. It is still a flower. It is still of essence, it still strives to be, and has feelings, emotions. I am speaking of your humans. Am I answering? Are you understanding? (Yes I am) Is it of help? (Yes)

So I then turn to you, and ask you not to be of judgement, for you cannot see the tapestry in full. You cannot see all of that, which is 'inter-played'. You say this 'inter-mixed'. The threads, the fibres all have a purpose and vibrate within the colour, the hues, and some choose the part. Remember upon one time we spoke of actors on stage, yes? Well it is of this ilk I am speaking to you. This life of yours here, most all is illusion. You know this, yes? Lose your judgement, I say. Give these situations the love freely, and allow them to be for the 'highest and best' for the lessons, of which are set there for those to learn it. And trust, again have faith, that it is set there for this, and it is serving purpose for good. Be lifted. Do not be downcast. Will this suffice for you? (Yes) Has it eased your mind for you? (Yes it has) Ah we have succeeded! Ah our pleasure.

(Asking along the same subject, the lessons you mentioned being allowed are not just applied to the people who committed the crime, but to the victims of that crime and their family?) It is hard to conceive, for these lessons seem to be so unfair to those who suffer, (Yes) for the 'hand of'. You, again you do not have the higher perspective to see that 'within all is a choice'. You say victim has no choice, no! You say that young child murdered—no choice! I am saying **all** has choice, not always conscious.

(Choice was made before they were born?) Ah, and during life it can be taken up. (I understand that, thanks) Ah that was easy. She is happy now!

(9-8-06)

... This requires an understanding of how important—as I have been speaking here this evening quite often: of your mind sets, of lifting above your fear-base, of what you believe, of how you walk upon the earth, of how well you are walking as a human being—for you do not realise what **great** effect it has upon all-that-which-is.

We have touched upon it when I speak of the fulcrum of now, of which you are, as having great effect upon all your pasts and futures. I have touched upon it, not this evening, but in various other venues, of which you are creating your 'New Age' you call it. How important it is for you to reach for the highest and best of that which you can be, for this is what you shall be existing within—within this New Age. The higher you lift, the higher you change—the fulcrum of the wind of change increases.

Ah, this is basically the essence of the answer. What you are affects all-that-is. So therefore, all you need do is to strive to be as the highest and best, and to accept that is what you are, and what is. It affects all the material, all of your relationships: your relationship with yourself, with your guidance of your spirit. It affects all that which comes to you, and that of which you experience.

You must remember that all experience upon this earth is not set to you. There are many that live within this earth, within this reality of which you share. You know that I speak of relativity a great deal, of this and not-that. That there are many lessons for the "that and not-this", of which you are. But in truth the this, of that which you are at the now, of which you experience, has great effect for that which is *not* you, for you shine as a beacon do you not, as a burning brightness to show the way of that which-can-be. You think that those who are . . . that have their heads turned do not notice in the darkness your light? And I assure you that it is noted. As moths to a flame, they are attracted, but at times are fearful of it. Is this answering in any way? (Yes I think so, a lot to take on and understand. Just simple things, keep away the other influences, and see it just as simply the light you carry. You are just that light and try to understand what effect it does have) It does (and accepts) Yes, and to trust that it has great healing properties. It has a great wisdom, great power of creating that-which-can-be, of that which you have desire for.

In a way you walk as a horse with blinkers. You walk steadfastly upon your path, but not without compassion, not without the love for the other, knowing that indeed just as your fear-base is part of you and you cannot separate, as I use the expression 'a cankerous limb', that those who are around you are being as they are, as they-can-be, as all is. And all of that which is the universe has the variety of that which is the crystal of many facets of the truth of that which they are, and this is infinite. So revel in the variety, and send love and compassion, and do not judge any of it, no matter how preposterous, 'evil' you say it appears. (Thanks) Our pleasure, we still are not sure if we have answered you quite as you would have hoped. (You have answered the question I should have asked) This is what I was meaning. We have not actually answered your question you asked, but we answered what you were asking. (Thanks) We hope this was satisfactory. We tend to make little jumps you see, and we are never sure if the fence was too high.

(20-10-07)

First and foremost we would like to remind you that all lessons set here upon the earth are not for your learning. There are many who co-inhabit this earthly plane with you. You know this. Not all actions and deeds that beset you are there, believe it or not, for your learning, and just are there for others. You are not the fulcrum of all-that-is, regarding all that besets those, your environment, and that which surrounds you.

Now I have gone on in the past, talked at great length regarding: yes you are the fulcrum of all-that-is. It is true, but it is also a case of it is . . . it is not a case that either/or. It is both. I have spoken many times of this, as in that you are your own focus within your own consciousness and also you are all-that-is, that you are everything and also a tiny bit of it.

So therefore in those experiences that you come across in your lives, such as this hardship that you have had to endure, it is not something that is directed at you. It is part of all-that-is, and not necessarily your focus that has caused it. (Right) At times you feel that it is in some way a part of your having caused it for some reason, yes? (Yes) We know this. We are being very careful with our words here, and gentle I hope.

(8-8-05)

(So does that mean if somebody does terrible deeds in the world, they have chosen to come back and do that for the benefit of others?) At times indeed yes at times indeed, at times—other times it is more to do with their mind sets and beliefs. For them it is of great reasoning for them to do this. They magnetise then those who want this lesson from them, and together they produce this picture. You understand? (I understand, but find it quite difficult as

we are taught to lead a life that is good.) Your relativity—
'good bad', you see you are still wrapped up within that.
(Sorry) You cannot help but be. You live here!

As in the temptation I began with you first of all your
negative opinion of: Ah well that is the devil beckoning
me to do the sins! (Yes) We are saying all is experience.
We do not judge. We do not see 'good-bad'. We see
experience. We see experience and intent. I have spoken
to you of intent, have I not, (Yes, many times) many
times. These are important.

And also you must remember that, as I stated once that
there was like the play, all have parts and the parts must
be taken. Once you are out of this relativity experience,
then you have no need. It is much different. Will that
suffice?

(Well I accept unconditional love for people, but
it is difficult when you are trying to lead a life and
understand. When things happen that makes others
suffer, are we just to accept that those souls who have
agreed to be the victims, or possibly-) I do not ask you to
take your compassion away. I never asked you to do that.
I do not ask you to take your healing thoughts away. I do
not ask you to stand upon the hill of a 'saintly spiritual
sort' who—"Oh my goodness that has nothing to do with
me! I am beyond that." No, no.

Remember that you are all creating this world as a
whole—all of mankind and you are a part of that. What

I do ask you is yes: to release your judgement, to walk within the unconditional love. And although you have not been explained the internalised belief system of that individual, for which it makes perfect sense for that one to do this, that you **cannot** understand it, for all is so **unique** within that which they are—their mind sets, their beliefs.

So all of you are walking within your 'individual bubble' let us say, with your glasses of coloured frames to see life as you do, and that is how it is, and it can be no different. And every one of you is different, and all the same. It is difficult to comprehend.

And yes we do ask you: to set aside your judgement, to set aside your 'good/bad', to set aside your relativity, for in truth it is not there. You cannot help but walk within it, but you can also know that it is an illusion.

This you must learn to do, for you to remain risen over your fears, for otherwise the fear-base shall be caught up, and it shall point to more and more in your life and say "Ah you have moved from my position! I told you I was right." Yes, that part of you which is fearful.

So it takes great bravery, strength of purpose, and a certain discipline for you to engage within your mind this sense that: it all has purpose. I cannot understand it. I cannot perceive it, for this within which I am living of relativity, but I have my spirit friends who shall help me for they have the higher perspective.

And we then turn, of course to remind you: to connect, to go to them, to ask for help in these times to help with understanding, to leave your judgement aside. You still live unconditional love, but unconditional love is not truly seen upon the earth. It cannot be, for it is of relativity. It is ... we do not know of one who lives with this here truly. You are also here to learn of love. That is what is. (Yes) Yes, will that suffice for you now? (Yes thanks) Happier now he is ... our pleasure.

Love and Happiness
(27-1-14)

Unconditional love—It is one of the reasons that you live upon this earth is to learn more about love. In fact it is one of the reasons all consciousness exists is to learn more about love, for it makes the all—everything!

(15-6-05)

Ah yes now ah ha, I like my amusing beginnings! You know of the 'golden egg' of which your magic chicken lays, of which your storybooks say of great ... hard work for the reaching and to pocket it? You think of happiness like this! That which you strive for, that which is nearly unobtainable and once you have it, you must: covet it, hide it away, and keep it close to you. Happiness is meant for the sharing, for the exuding outwards, as of a light, which shines as a beacon. Not to put in pocket, no. Not to store away.

Now I have spoken to you upon the link of the joy, of which all mankind is human. The right, the birth right, of which you are vying to reach this golden egg your pathway is taking you to for . . . how can I repeat this again for you . . . for you to grasp it firmly?

You are here to lift above your fears, to connect with your spirit. In lifting up of your fears and your connection with spirit, you then walk freely forward. You place your highest and best in front, and your feet shall fall only there. You then walk within peace and freedom, and you will find that the joy of which you walk is ever there, for you become of faith and trust that it is truly so, for you understand **with** the aide of your guidance from spirit, with the higher perspective, that all is set there for reason: for improvement, for lessons, for—yes, for the lifting of your fellow man, for the consciousness to experience, to expand. Is this not joyous, all of this?

You are learning to be of more love. This is part of your joyousness, of your happiness, is it not? For it is so keenly attached, you cannot in actuality separate it, as with a knife. They are as one. So you go along in your life and learn of love. You have your relationships. You have your friendships. You have that love of your pets, your animals, your gardens, yes your food—you can go on and list . . .
—TURN TAPE-

I will pause here and see if you have questions of this.
Is this what you were asking of me? (Yeah) I believe it
pertains to you all, for you feel that this golden egg is
something that is such hard work, that is just out of reach,
and once reached, you must keep so carefully for fear that
it will be broken, for in truth your happiness is broken.
Your love gets broken. You feel it—this in your heart, for
your relationships may fail. Things are not quite right,
and you become 'unhappy'.

It does not behove anyone for you to say problem, and
then take it as yours. It is their problem. It is their life. You
can set highest and best. You can set healing to it. You can
set love to it, but the healing only if it is set to highest and
best for their path. Not because you want them cured in
some way. Not because you wish them to be without this.
Not because you even wish their problem to be resolved
for them. You can set your love and highest and best, the
healing light just to be as light for their pathway. And
not many of you healers do that upon this earth, for they
feel that they need to send (I am rattling his cage) they
feel they need to send that healing as to how *they* would
perceive. It needs to be freely given. These things are set
as a reminder that . . . oh dear.

We know that you know that you are all connected. You
are all in touch with let's say, an electric static coming off.
It does not mean that you take their energy in as yours.
You have your own, and only through your own energy

and using that link with spirit and sent out as freely as highest and best, will it be of any benefit. I am not doing a very good job of this. Hah

You are all unique, yes you know this. You are all individual. You have your own power point. You have your own fulcrum of time, of which is now, you

This is an existence, of which you are of the learning, for you to expand from your sense of knowing, of knowledge of your beliefs: of how you see the world, of how you see yourselves and others, for you to increase that knowledge of self, to look within, yes indeed, and to find its reflection without, indeed.

For us in spirit, we are not of unhappiness. We are of happiness. It 'saddens us at times'. We use this phrase of words, but in truth we are of joy, of love. This is what you are of. It is because you live within this illusory relativity of which you bespeak of your earth—you know of it as, and you see this illusion and you feel enmeshed, and your egg is broken.

The egg cannot be broken. The egg in truth lies deep within your heart and is always with you. You need not climb. You need not strive. All you need to do is to be of this. Just to be of this, as the plants, the animals, yes to exist within the joy, the peace and the happiness, the love of which you are truly! The rest is illusion! (Yeah)

Now I shall pause once more and ask if you have questions. (No more) So you are understanding more now how this relates. Why I begin with 'egg' of golden. You find golden a high colour—spiritual. Well you are of that **now**! And you know I have spoken of when you feel the egg is broken, well there are lessons for returning to that: to know and to re-choose that which you wish to be. This, your earth gives you and provides for you, so freely and so lovingly.

Healing/Helping
(9-12-12)

(We are responsible for self only, but intertwine with others on earth and wish to fix their problems)

Because it pulls at their hearts, they feel that they need to fix it, to help it, or else they would not be spiritual people would they? It is also to do with their love. It is part of doing with being human in that if someone comes, saying: I have a problem. You feel that you must fix problem. Instead of saying: you have a problem, and say: um problem. That is an interesting problem. It is your problem isn't it. Let's sit down and look at it together. It is still your problem. I do not . . . ah I know.

This one we spoke to her many, many years ago of not taking the beasts to the table of others. In other words, you do not . . . ah that was an aside.[1] (Reference "Beasts at Table" 25-12-92)

---

[1] BEASTS AT THE TABLE (25-12-92)

Best hit at the beasts that live in mind of many. One can know the nature of the beast, but little can be done in the minds of others if they choose to dine with them . . . bemoaning the bad manners and fearsome appetites of *their* guest, but not lifting a finger to demand their transmutations which would free them of these loathsome guests. Hit upon the thoughts, but do not carry them home to sup from your table, to release the apparent sufferer! No service is in this, as it robs the other of the lesson. Time is on everyone's side, if they but use it wisely.

Forge a link to different beings and learn. Trust in finding the answers as needed and do not concern yourself that Light does not have it ALL in hand! Be a friend. Be kind and giving. Learn that some are so young, that lessons are not learned quickly in even these times.

So be of good counsel, but do not expect to be heard by many. In this wisdom, be giving but do not tarry with those who choose the beasts at the table to new creatures/creations of thought. The mind holds tightly to patterns and fears changes. Instead, free Light from hearts by kindling companionship in many. Be a beast tamer **for self** only, but teach others by deeds and thoughts. They will take the seed and seasons must pass for firm roots to grow to support the new manifestation that is fast coming to earth.

Harbingers of spring give promise of new growth, even after the longest of winters. Be thus. Be prepared. The winter shall turn to spring. The darkness shall be given up into the LIGHT. Rest assured in this. Life is for now. So be in tune and play sweetly. The sweeter the tune today, the higher the path will carry. Those who become sour in tastes and attitude choose the company of their table companions a while longer still. Fret not . . . the fearsome beasties are angelic in disguise! They do not mean harm, only lessons for their creators.

Kindred spirits will come one's way once lessons gifted in present companions are well learned. Think of these times as beginnings in TRUST . . . do trust in us and go peacefully as a beacon too many in these troubled times. Forge a New Age for those who choose it. Be of good spirit's company, if those around you are unwise and foolish. Ponder the reasoning behind it, do not be partner to it. Boundaries are wise in such times, so use Light to surround self, when in company of such. We are close! *TRUST*!!!

Standing there. It does not mean—no man is an island. It does not mean that you are not touching on other's energies-yes, love. We are trying this again! It all is affecting you, because it touches your heart. It does not mean that you lose yourself in trying to resolve, or be another, or be something else for the other. Yes you have heard these words before, and how many of you do it time and time again. It is part of the social patterning within your mind almost to strive to be what the other wishes. We are asking you to be brave enough and strong enough to hold the torch of light and say: this is me! Now am I making it clearer?

Not an easy thing to do in this world we know, and we do not ask you to do it at all times, but that is what you are striving to be is just you. Not that person's problems, not that one's problems, not such because that one might be able to fit in that group a bit better if, yes? Or—you know where all these pressures come from. Not because you think you know love, and that you cannot let this one go because it would mean-because of the fear, or because of not understanding what love is, which none of you do here upon this earth, in truth.

This is one of the-I wish almost to use the word shocks that you'll come upon when you open more fully to that which is coming into your world, of which you are creating, as the intensity of the love that you have no idea of. And you cannot enjoy that purely when you are living not-as-you in any form . . . do you understand that expression not-as-you . . . because that love has to do with love of yourself first and foremost . . . "Oh mustn't do that" . . . because that is where it burns the brightest, and then it shines out and affects and touches, as again a fulcrum to all-that-is. It teaches others, and they will be drawn to you, for you shall be shining with light. And that light also will be, not only a beacon for others upon the earth, but also a beacon to this future energy, yes which is on its way, and is here, and then you will be as-one with it.

Reincarnation/Guides
(19-7-07)

Mankind has a great misunderstanding of reincarnation. There is some belief that it passes through all of the animal kingdom and comes up to the 'higher level of mankind'. Well, we are here to disappoint you. It is your choice at your birth whether you partake in being part of a tree, a stone, or a human being, or a dog or a stick insect. It is your choice of that which you desire to experience. You are free to use your consciousness, as you will. It is called freedom of choice.

Now here, you have chosen this one unusual beast called a human being in this lifetime. Now we ask you, in that which you inhabit your soul part that you call your consciousness, that you usually attach yourself, upon your death you do not take your body with you, do you? No. And what do you inhabit in this bodily form? What is it made up from? It is made up from the bits of the dog and the tree, of the earth, the stardust, and it is a part of you, because you have inhabited within it and it inhabits with you.

I am pointing out to you that your physical body is an essence of that which is the consciousness, of which all things are made up of. You have to understand that within your earth is a fabric: within your molecules, within your smallest, within your quantum physics you are brought into this dimension to then become material. This includes the dog, the man. It then allows you to inhabit this and that of which the parts then become a whole, become a part of you and cohabit with that soul essence, of which you have decided to send down from your higher self.

The amount of times people speak of: oh that is an old soul. Oh that is a new soul. It really makes no difference how many times you inhabit the earth as to the oldness and newness of you. It is simply the focus of which you have chosen to come with.

(9-12-12)

(Who is my guide?)Many of the energies will come from many lives and present as different lifetimes—the same energy. You may have Indian, and then the same energy will be an old sailor. You have off world. It could be an energy also of that which had lived here, which you knew before previously, but which has now come in as an off world existence to you for you feel more comfortable and at ease. You have gotten to know better. This is how spirit works to build up the guide relationship.

(25-1-07)

(How do I find my guide?) The pathway is the same for all humankind. I do not need to speak with them, for the answer is the same, although they are with me. The answer is the same for all mankind is that: it is a road of discovery.

You must first discover how you yourself work. You do not know yourself. You think you do, but you do not know. Some will hear a voice. Some will never hear a voice, but will have an intuitive knowledge. They will see images. Thoughts will come into their mind. They will dismiss it all and say: ah that was not spirit.

So upon this road, upon this path there are steps along it as she . . . You acknowledge that spirit is actually there. You acknowledge that you are actually requesting, which we realise that you are, that they are actually responding to you, and to allow yourself time: to get to know each other, to gain a familiarity.

Now many people will say: now who is my guide? Yes well oh dear. You must realise that here I am. I come as I am for familiarity, not only for this one here, for she would be most uncomfortable if I came within a different life each and every time, and it would be most confusing for you who come to listen to me, for you would not feel comfortable.

So therefore, it is a pathway of getting to know that which you are . . . freewill. Happy within all the incarnations of that guide who will be as-one with you, you then have free choice for you to agree upon an incarnation of which you feel comfortable. I keep repeating 'comfortable'. Well you understanding me? (Yes)

So this takes a time. So one day you may feel you may have a nun, and another day a monk or whatever. They could be all the same spirit energy yes, confusing isn't it? Allow it to be confusing, and allow yourself to find comfort in . . . again you must build in your trust and faith. That is the biggest teaching we have, they have, for you.

You have asked. They are answering you, blowing their horns in a great loud noise. I do not know what else to say. It echoes all around you, and you cannot hear the din, for you have not the faith and trust to take it up, for ears to open, your eyes and your feeling, your senses, which takes time. So it is . . . this one calls it a dear friend called "Percy" . . . perseverance. That is her joke. You must persevere. Walk the road. It is long, and it can be very short.

But the first steps is having a heart-felt *knowing* that they are there, *trusting* that they are there, and *asking* at every point in your life for them to be a part of yours. That is our answer for you at this moment of your progression, your ascendancy up the ladder.

(2-7-12)

First of all to use us, to acknowledge us, well that is the
beginning steps. It is like all the things, the more that
you use it, the stronger it becomes, the easier it becomes
obviously. To strengthen that helps and it would improve,
help all of you in more ways than just within your spirit
communications. Quieten your minds. You understand.
Your minds are so busy with this, that, this hum . . . busy,
busy . . . to have a quiet mind. You know you say of a stone
dropping into the pond, the ripples? Yes well that would
be the spirit, and you would require a mind of stillness.

Now we understand that none of you will be able to do
that "24 hours of the 7" you say in that expression. We
would not expect that in the beginning, but

towards your . . . it would be a goal to set, your objective
to be able to stay within a stone's throw, a breath away for
us to be with you as-one.

(20-10-07)

You are asking about spirit guides yes. (Yes) You are
asking about your spirit guides as well. You are asking
about humanity's spirit guides. Well I say it is the right
of every one of you, and you all have your own spirit
guides. You are asking about the process of how they
are chosen. Well I say they are chosen before you come
to this conception, before you have chosen which foetal

mass that you shall attach yourself to: the genetic codes, the parenting, and the chances of events occurring. And here you are. You have already agreed before you have come that your loved ones in the spirit word, one will be as-one with you, and there will be many who . . . um again you have to understand that your spirit guides, that the people can pop in and out as to your focus, as to their focus. They will be magnetised to what you are doing. And also too your guides can change, as you change and develop and grow within your own experiences. Stop me at any point. I shall just keep going.

So therefore you arrive upon the earth. You are growing up, but we don't expect too much from children, but at times they are more adept than most of your grownups I might say, and most definitely. But let us pretend that you are one of these children, who is very veiled and who has no memory. Although you have promised from the depths of your heart that you will not forget, that how could you forget this love-bind, bond agreement before you came to this earth with your loved ones, your guides who have agreed to be your guides, shaken hands, contracts signed. Ah: imagination, they are not there! Who are they? I do not remember. I haven't got any? Ah, on it goes. You know the script. –Laughter—And here we are in spirit going: hello! Yes we are here. You have asked for proof and here we have provided it and provided it, and you, like with the eraser on the black board, you rub it out: imagination. That's just, that's just.

And so you come along your path, and come along this path into this group. You decide to take it more seriously, and begin to allow yourself, ah ha key words 'to allow yourself' to not only entertain, but to *accept* the fact that perhaps that this is not just imagination. That in truth you are speaking to your guides: ah um, oh dear am I crazy? Over to this gentleman please in a neatly queue!

So here you are: who is my guide? Your next question is it not. Well it usually is for beginners. So we then go through this explanation that well—I come within my Indian form. I could come as different format of a human being each visit and oh, you would be lost. You would not have the familiarity, would you? This one would not, who sits here with me. She would not be happy at all.

So therefore, it is freewill and choice therefore upon the earthly plane as well, to work with this light of spirit, for them to join within a format which is a pleasing combination for you to accept and be familiar with and able to receive. (Thanks) So it is not set in stone: it is a Chinese or lady, yes? No, no I am sorry to disappoint you. (It answers a lot actually.) Good, good, it is a process. Allow it to be, and enjoy the journey, for you are creating with your spirit guides, and they revel in it when you finally turn to the light and allow this to be. Ah they are finally being heard! Great rejoice, yes. (Thanks) Pleasure, was that enough for you? I could continue. Better give others a chance eh!

(19-7-07)

(Giving a workshop on connecting to guides, any advice?) Ah you know what box I shall stand upon, my favourite soapbox, and here I clamber upon it again. I would advise you to ask them to look at what they fear, what's holding them back, why they have to go to this workshop, for to doing what is the human

right. The natural way of being a human being upon this earth is to be in connection with spirit at all times, yes and here they have to go to a workshop to learn, and think: Ach am I able? Let us have a go. Oh they know how, I do not. I . . . yes? Oh my.

So this is where we would begin is to ask them to hold a mirror up to themselves. To ask them to see what they themselves appear on the **other** side of the mirror looking at them. To consider that that is spirit on the other side of the mirror, and when **they** are looking at the mirror, all they are looking at is **they**!

Most people have a mirror in their pockets, yes? You can bring some along, and then ask them why spirit has such a hard time communicating with them, when all they are doing is looking at that mirror, and throwing their fears at it, and bouncing it back at themselves? And then ask them what they would do to then pass through that mirror to dissolve it, so that they can actually: see, hear, feel, sense, be with their guides, who are ever with them.

And then, you can take the step into the second stage, of then **how** they would go about that. And you know that would involve asking of course, allowing, trusting—'Is this my imagination?'—Practise, perseverance, yes? And then their feet are upon the road. Has that sufficed for you? (Thanks) Pleasure. (I'll bring some mirrors) Remember the teaching though, that of my soapbox, is always to raise above the fears, and this is part and parcel of that, which the human has come to earth for to learn: to lift above the fears, to lift to spirit, to lift above the fears to find the pure freedom of the joy and the peace . . . true peace of mind, which is their right. That will suffice, or I shall go on and on. Ah you know how I am!

TIME

(10-5-01) Much is spoken of time, we could elaborate. Well, I'm considering a chicken's egg. You consider it takes time—takes time to be a chicken: to develop within the shell, to crack the shell, to come out and grow, to lay another egg. This is a sequence of time. It is very difficult for you to consider that this is actually all in 'one time' as it were. The thought, the 'intention', again I refer to that. This is my understanding I am giving to you is this egg would be a chicken. Yes it is designed and set that way in this space and time. It appears to take time, but in actual fact it is very, very rapid. So rapid there is no time really involved. It is the thought of the chicken to be that egg to be a chicken. That is what is involved. You think that chick in the egg has no thought, or the chicken as a chicken has no thought. I am saying: yes, perhaps the thought of the chicken drives that chick to be that chicken it will be, yes? Confusing? No not really.

We could take an example of a flower. That is often used. You think yourself when you plant a garden, you plant a little corm or a bulb and you imagine the flower, do you not? Do you not think that has a great effect on that flower? It does. You know so. That flower also has an effect on the bulb and the corm to become that flower as well.

It is the 'intention'. The intention is slowed on this Earth plane in this world. So it looks, appears to take time. This is why your Spirit friend speaks of being so quick, 'no time at all'. That would be very nice wouldn't it? Then you would have no problem with time. You actually do not. You only appear and feel that you do, because things are so sluggish.

What's important is to take time to remember to put the intention of where you want to be and go in that space of time. You will get there quicker. You know this. So it might be wise if you're impatient and finding you are not getting somewhere quick enough, not having time to do something, to take time to get yourself there quicker, by pretending and thinking that you are there, like planting the flower perhaps.

Do you understand? Well practise this. Practise this more. It is the essence of how things come to be in our world as it is in yours, although it appears much slower as it is in yours, although it is all like this. So spend time considering your intention and quality of all you want to be.

(31-5-01)

There are multiple forms, many worlds, many ways and places and states of being. This is one of, I want to state, the lesser. I do not want to sound hurtful. Remember the dog's tail? I'm thinking on fleas. As if that one flea on that dog was all that she knew, being the flea. She does not realise that she is even on the dog, that flea. I am talking of her, as the flea.

I am saying that your life here is so veiled in forgetfulness that you do not realise the bigger extent, and see only this as all. And some adamantly refuse to consider that they could possibly be less than all, as your theories at one time had the planets revolving around the Earth. We know different now, yes I hope? OK.

Many people are like this still. They think that, regard that they are the hub of the universe. In a way they are, but they forget—again back to the dog being the dog— the tail of the dog—the tip of the tail is not the whole dog. It would be absurd to think that the flea on the dog was the whole dog as well. Yes? People think this. I am saying that you are all very large dogs, yes with: many fleas, many lives being lead, many focuses on one life, which is the dog. This is the point I am trying to make. Each flea has a different spot to chew and the dog has many fleas to chew on, and the perspectives are different but the same as to the dog. Do you understand this?

Now, if you can accept this concept, then perhaps you can consider that your life is many and varied, as to the perspective of the one life that is lived, this being only one **small** facet to be considered.

(27-01-14)

First off may we remind you where I began that the fulcrum of time is now, that you have a spot that you focus upon? It is your focus that produces. Your mind sets and beliefs is a focus. That is what creates what is for you. Now know that the reality is infinite, yes I would hope, that love is infinite. Love is knowing itself by focusing here, there, everywhere. There are many levels. So it splits itself and tries a "this/not that" for learning to know itself, to remember who it is, what it wishes to be, how to go back to that source of being just that.

As you live your lives, you have considered that when you die you may return. You have considered that you have lived—we have discussed past lives, so you consider that you have lived many times here upon this earth plane. I know I have. That is why I am chosen as spokesperson, for I have lived here many lives. But seldom do you consider that you have lived many lives elsewhere besides this planet, upon earth.

Seldom do you think when you are working on a problem that the future has as much power that you can utilise as your past. You say: how can I increase my consciousness, my spiritual energy? Well ask your future self, who has already gotten there, and ask yourself to become that.

There are many things that can be done when you realise that

All time is now. You can, as I stated

Here, access your other lives that are living in tandem with you. In truth . . . ah they want me to explain this first.

In earth you like this concept: well it is that or this. Yes that is the problem of living in relativity because you are so used to good/bad, this/not that . . . not this I mean, that seldom do you consider in context, in a format of both. So something is a focus, as you know your life to be. Your mind sets, values, beliefs are the creation of which you live around you, but you are also that of your higher self. You are also that of the lives that are living in other dimensions simultaneously and you are also all-that-is. So you are both, everything, and this small focus. You understanding me? I have tried to make it more easy for you to grasp.

(29-6-07)

First of all I would like to point out that which I have spoken many times of before, but you have not heard, so I shall repeat. I told you we were very good at repetition! Here I go.

Ah, that which you are now is the fulcrum of all of what is, in the future and past. All is now. There is no future and past. It is all now. Now that is a very difficult and impossible concept for you to take on within this human shell of, within this relativity-based earthly life, you understanding me. You cannot possibly take up this full understanding, but you ask and I say. So all time is now, so again we repeat—me on my box of soap I go again—with the request, with the oh . . . beseeching of your guides for you to be lifted above your fear-base, and to be as highly and best set upon your path, setting there your footprints, are putting them there.

So what does that suggest? You are also led from the future, as from the past. Your now-of-yourself reflects and affects all that is, that is you. So therefore you are you: within the unique self as you, within the consciousness of your existence here upon the earthly. You are also your higher self. You are also all of the existences of which you can live: within all the dimensions of earthly and all other life. Life, well you would not know it as life, of consciousness, of which you . . .

I do not know why human on earth makes it so small for life only to be of material or physical. They are so sadly mistaken. It is everywhere. It is light. It is called love. It permeates and it is all of what is. So therefore within your unique self you are that part, and also you are all of it, *all of it*!

So you ask me reincarnation, and so how will I answer? I will answer in that you are living a now of which you have an effect upon all that which is. And so in essence you are all of your incarnations that all that consciousness could possibly experience. It is for experience that you are to experience self, to be. Will that suffice for you? Has that explained? (Yes) Think about it. If you wish to come back to me I am happy to clear up. I make muddy puddles, and sometimes you can see so clearly, and I stir it all up. Oh dear. It is difficult for us, for us to use your words within the consciousness of that earthly you that you are, for us to explain our spirit perspective. (Yes) Pleasure. Consider and return. (Will do)

(14-2-08)

(Similar to before and all the dimensions and any one time we are here, but also in others. Is it possible if there are more than one of us here at once, and when you meet someone who stands out to you are they part of you or your soul family?) In truth all of humanity who is upon the earth and who is in spirit is your soul family. You know this. And all of the material, of which the earth is made from, is part of your soul family. You consider consciousness just within your humanity yes, or perhaps some of your animals, but we say again it is made up of even the spaces between the atoms. It . . . all has a wish to grow, to expand, to experience—life force. Ah.

Again we come to the spot on the floor do we not. (Thought you might) Yes it is still there. And you are seeing as: this is me. And there is another spot there. Spots are looking up, and seeing the stars are there. And seeing that as your fellow and different countries, and yes forgetting because you are within it, that to go "meta" you say, to go and realise that you are just part, and also you are . . . within your chakra vibrational levels, good way to state it, for lack of definition . . . that you are also the whole.

So yes indeed each person that you meet, we encourage you to greet them as part of you, for indeed they are. Each tree, each people, each mote of dust, each draft of wind upon/through your hair, upon your face is part of you. (Thanks) And greet them as brothers. Greet them as sisters, mothers, fathers, yourself, and listen. Be in tune with them yes, and to not pass judgement. To allow them to be just as they are with love sent to them, all of it.

Again this comes back and harking back to what I keep upon my box of soap, one of my most important things we have to say to you is to remind you to place that love to the highest and the best to all-that-is, regardless its

appearance, and allow it to be. Try not to describe and
assign to it your concepts. Ah they are saying shush. You
are going beyond what she asked. I have answered you
in truth. (I understand) Pleasure. I need an on off button
like the machine!

(19-7-07)

(Is there a connecting thread concerning past and future
lives, as it appears not to be) Oh you know there is. We
have taught you this. The now! You do not understand,
no. The now is the fulcrum of all-that-is. Now you know
that that now, it appears to be constantly in change:
future, pasts, and different dimensions. So now there is
no time.

Now the connection, from what thread you are now
looking at is from the aspect of your earth-bound
perspective, in which you have time, relativity . . . this/
not that, you know all of that. So therefore when you
look upon your reincarnations, perhaps you do past
life—'past life'—Always past life, why not future life—
then regressions, aggressions, no, no it would not be
aggressions. What would be the right word? No, no I
do not think there is one. Is there? Anyway back to the
business.

It is your consciousness. Again what you are in the now is
what affects all-that-is. This is why we go on and on so: for
being lifted above your fears, for reaching that peace of

mind, to be as-one with your spirit guides, placing *all* to highest and best, for this has an effect on **all**. This is called mastery, is it not?

And once you become and learn to become a master of one life, then all that you are—you have such great affect, greater affect, more positive—you say 'positive/negative', your relativity, the now-of-which—all-that-is exists around you within and without, yes all-that-is. (Sorry I asked) No (I recognise the answer) Do you recognise the answer? (I do) You do indeed. (Sorry about that) That's all right. I do not need to go on. Would you like for me to continue, or will that suffice? (-) Suffice yes I shall zip it.

(Hello LS) Good evening I am allowed to speak to you, not him! (Do you think-?-) Simplified, this one was further advanced. Simplified, ah let us see. (All time is now is what you are saying? Some did not understand. Try again.) I understand that. This is the difficulty of having a miss match . . . mishmash—oh your words.

Well I would like to start with relativity I believe, for them to understand that their earth-base is of relativity, and for them to understand what relativity is. So therefore it is this-not-that, good/bad, yes. So this is there for you to understand what you are, to remember what you are, to remember that you have choice, and to remember, and re-choose. To be master of the fear-base you must have the fear-base, for that is the relativity of the higher set mastered self, of your higher self, yes understood?

Step 2: once you have a grasp of, then you realise that your earth bound base of your existence is not all that you are. You have your higher self.

Step 3: now you have your higher self. What is that composed of? It is part of you here. What else is it? I would suggest it is as the embers of a fire cast out, as a log will explode, the embers will cast out upon the grass and be as your other lives, as a firework will explode in the sky—other lives, multitudinous, understood?

Where are we Step 4? We shall stop counting. Now consider that. You feel that you look upon the firework in the sky, and say: yes this ember, that, that rocket, that firework is me, the essence of me, my higher self and exploded in all your lives: the past lives, your future lives, the lives not only within this dimension, but all the dimensions—ah this is where we are coming to— dimensionality. You are only looking at that firework from your earth-bound relativity base. If perceived from your higher self, from the spirit would find that that firework resounded much further into other dimensions, of which you cannot perceive from your earth bound perspective, understood? Um not so much so, ah . . . You must stretch your mind to this.

What we are saying is that you consider what you live on this earth as all that exists. You then know that there is spirit. You contact and you think: ah there is something else. You forget that you are also existing within this spirit world. You are existing within all the dimensionalities, and you are in fact all-that-is, and the small part of which you are. This is called focus.

This means that you are all all-that-is, the whole kit and caboodle of the universe is contained within the minute focus of you within this earth-plane. And it is only this focus, of which becomes all of your lives, all that you are, becomes the gestalt of all-that-is, and understood? You asked me to explain. I am trying! So therefore time— how can time be of a true existence when all of your lives are lived at once? Interconnected you are all, and you are all the parcels—you are all that exists.

What is consciousness but a desire to grow? It exists within the minutest spark of the existence of that-which-is. It is within your fabric of your material, and you say: oh it does not live. It has no consciousness of thought. You know nothing of what consciousness is of. You believe this. Your body has a consciousness. Your material body has consciousness, and it is in a different consciousness of that which . . . ah we will not go there. No that is too much. They are telling me: no, no concentrate on the path. Are we getting anywhere further though along the road of getting you to understand that all time is now?

So therefore if that firework in the sky seen from your earth-base, you can perceive that all of those sparks of the lives of which you can perceive from *your* focus of *your* earth-bound life that you are *now within this focus,* you can then lift and look from your higher self and all

the lives of which all those fireworks are exploding in
the universe around within all of the time, dimensions,
and yes, you get a greater and grander picture. You
become aware that you are all-of-one, and how can that
be separated in truth into parts, when really in truth it is
as-one.

This is why we are telling you not to judge, not to be
critical for that friend you have fallen out with is a part of
you. You have fallen out with yourself. This is why we ask
you to be loving and non-judgemental and not critical for
all that happens and goes on within and upon your earth
and within yourself. This is why it is such a good learning
space for you have your fear-base. You wish to cut it away.
You think it ugly that you have fear, that things happen
within your world that are less than 'good', less than of
the best you see, but they are there for a true teaching for
you and should be blessed and in truth are all of the light.
But that carries on to a new field. Will that suffice for you?
Has that helped? I/We hope so

New Age
(8-8-12)

I shall start this answer with the dreaded statement that
all time is now and start with bamboozling you with the
idea that the energies that are coming, the new world that
you perceive as in future, yes as in coming to you, not
here as yet, has already been, and is already now being.

So therefore what is happening is that, that which your consciousness is, as to the unique form of life of which is your spot on the floor is the casting out, a reflecting. It is a dance between the vibrations, let us say, to create that which is the now. Um we are losing you all. We are answering you in a complicated way. I shall simplify it. One moment, for some can understand the more complicated, ah we believe.

Therefore that, of which is sent as a vibration of energy, I have spoken of this before. It is that human upon the earth which attunes to it, and therefore is a part of that reality, you understanding. That vibration of New Age has always been. It takes therefore that which is humankind, either uniquely individually, or also as the gestalt of the all. As your body holds many organs and atoms, so mankind, as you understand it, is a group as well. It is creating for itself a group experience, and that group experience will change its rules, let us say for a simplistic word to use, of that which will be for it, again just as the individual does. Yes, we are getting there using very few words.

Now your question was basically along the lines of just how much is this energy interacting and changing. We are saying to you in this answer, that it is not so much the energy interacting that is changing it is you that is changing and becoming aware of that energy. So it is you that is changing. The energy is not necessarily changing you. It is you, as you increase your vibration, increase your consciousness, your understanding, your awareness yes all of this, then you become aware of it. And it seems as if it just appeared and it is having an effect upon you!

Now you know it is all, as a whole, yes. And also too you know that that flame of your soul is split into different unique spots on the floor for the experience. This is so that all-that-is can have experience and know itself in many ways. So, therefore as you go along, that which you are, of that awareness on that spot on the floor is the thing that changes. This is why we have always stated to you it is the fulcrum of the now which is the power point. It has an effect on all-that-is.

Hence we again encourage you to take the responsibility of that which you are yes: in your thoughts, in your beliefs, your heart, and your intent. Not that you do not, but to remind you all to take it most seriously, for consider that it does matter. Yes it matters to all-that-is: pasts, presents, futures. And that is where I shall leave that answer as a carrot to all, carrots in front of the donkey's noses. You see we cannot lead you. We cannot pick the donkey up and put it in a fresh field. You understand you being the donkey. We can only offer you temptations for you to go there of your own accord. Freewill

Mankind is a group, and as a group lifts. This time of which you consider as time of now, it has taken a long time to get here, for so many to become aware and lift, but to us, we remind you that within the world of spirit, within the reality of what really is, it is all now. So therefore again we repeat what is changing is that which is of the experience of earthly life. And the only ones who can change that/ alter it are those experiencing it in corporeal body.

(26-06-06)

(Sometimes I feel overwhelmed by the speed of life today. It seems to be getting faster and faster and um sometimes I don't know how to stop. Can you give me any help?) Do you understand why it is quicker, quickening? (Can you explain that to me?) That can take a lengthy dissertation. I am thinking of having to do it with a shorter time, for you all to ask your questions.

You understand your creative mode of the human being? How it operates? How you magnetise that which is for you to live, through your mind-sets, your thought? (Yes)

So you understand also the lifting above your fears, as we have been speaking? Before you . . . you would not wish to magnetise within your life that which is based upon fear, upon greed, etc., etc . . . all. You are looking for a more loving 'New Age', you call it, let us call it, for you to walk freer within the love of each other—unconditional, without such judgement of self and others. So you understand that you are drawing and focusing this New Age, you are creating it with what you are bringing to it **now**. You understand the importance of this, yes?

So therefore, how would we—would it have been wise if you were overlooking this relativity of earth, you understand relativity, of this-and-not-that, black/white, good/bad, of which you are set upon the earth within for reminding you who you are. A human being walking proudly, lifted above their fears, mastering of their life, mastering their fears and in contact with their higher self and their spirit guides at all times, as best lived here on earth at all times—no matter what it appears to be.

Understanding all that, if you were engaged in looking after this realm of consciousness, to be interacting within, would it be wise to allow them to create at the speed in spirit we do? I think not. It would be a terrible muddle, for you know that within your experience of yourself and others how quickly mankind upon this earth can switch and change and be so fearful and wrapped up, and what would you then be producing, you magnetising your lessons? You know that you have a focus of all of mankind. You are not only magnetising your individual lessons.

So therefore as the energy—the lifting of the vibrations . . . is 'lifting' you call it . . . then time will be swifter, for you are magnetising that which is for your experience at a quicker rate of speed, a notch up, a shifting of gear. You will be not at the rate of spirit, of which/in which—um how would you say that? "Of which", "in which" I reside, in which your guides are in your higher self. This small fragment of you, which is in this relativity, is a very tiny portion of that which you are, you understand?

(26-4-07)

I think one of the greatest differences, of which of course your New Age will also bring into issues here, is that of the time that you know of, of it altering, of it—You know in spirit you hear that um, oh goodness the earth would be in such a mess if you had our ability in spirit to think and be, for you upon this earth will one moment think: Oh yes I shall be doing thus and such, and the next moment it's: Oh I shall be doing thus and such. And what a mess it would be, would you not agree? It would digress all the rules, and the fabric could not hold. It would be such a confusion within this, hence we slow time for you for you to remember your responsibility, the importance of being lifted above your fears—Ah ha I am slipping upon my box of soap here ah ha to give you your lecture once again—to keep lifted, to keep as-one with your spirit guides, to remember to be human, to trust that this is your true path. Yes, but this is not answering the question, no it is not at all! So I must step down off of my box of soap. They are telling me off for standing up upon it again. Ah they are strict with me. They must I suppose, yes um.

(9-12-12)

(Upon asking for a group meditation for 21-12-12) Well
what I have spoken of is one of the most important. I have
spoken of lifting above your fears, of not expecting you
to be able to at all times, that you cannot cut it off like a
bad limb, that you send love, honour and respect for all
that is you, that which is and that which not-is. Funny
words, you know what I am saying: that which is of light
and that which is of fear-base and not so good, yes good/
not so good hierarchy. So we are asking you to strive and
achieve every day and at all times to find that quiet space
within to maintain and to hook, um to stay united as-one
with your spirit, of which you all do so well, but to do at
all times.

To remember to ask, you are co-creating with them, that
which is.

You speak of your path. Well we say your path is created
by you.

You speak of your achievements, your world, your New
Age, and we say you are co-creating that with spirit. It
is not only from placing highest and best, lifting up and
working with; it is also created from your mind sets and
beliefs. That is how all things are and you know this. I am
starting with basics and working up quickly.

Therefore, we ask what is of very most importance for you
to do at these times, that you know about already, is to

strive to be your highest and best at all times. To clear, to dust away, to lift above, all of these words. Yes, easy said and more difficult to do, especially when times are not conducive to such thinking. You know those times: the puddles, the deep holes, the well-trodden plains, in which you scurry about within your fenced area of: oh. Yes to lift above and love yourself for it, for remembering that you live in this relativity, this dichotomy of this/not that. So therefore because you are living here, you are made thus, and that is how it is.

Now you are striving to reach towards a um, New Age of 2012, of all these words, of co-creating an existence which is less sticky a substance of relativity, that is more free from it, that is more of light and love and less of the not so. You feel that you have chosen and you wish to create from that chosen point of light, to set it there upon all. And that is the important lesson of what you are manifesting of 2012. It is practice. It is showing that you have learnt from this lifetime that you have come back upon this Earth to be, to create something more for your consciousness to reside within.

This sound rather mundane, it sounds rather as if I am speaking what you all know. I know that you know it. I am trying to set in front of you the fact that what you are creating, you are creating not only in your groups, but as humans . . . as a group across the earth, you know this, but what I am saying is that you are creating another dimension with the help of spirit, another Age, another place to be. It has happened before. It happens again. It happens in future. All time is now . . . Aha I have put it in aha! I warned you that I would. There it is . . . But all time is now—yes, your fulcrum.

I put that there to say that the fulcrum of your power point is *now*. It is this spot on the floor, in which you have incarnated within. You know that you live elsewhere. You know that you have contacts with other lives, within future and past. You know that you can help call for from future to help bring, pull yourself to. It works both ways. You know that this fulcrum-of-the-now point of which you are affects all-that-is: pasts, futures—all that is.

So you ask me what the most important thing for you to meditate on and I would say to remind yourself of the importance of what you are now, for often you think of your world and you think of what you perceive as the universe and you find yourself very small. You think you do not matter. Is this group worth going on?

Oh this . . . we say that you matter so much, for it is you that are affecting everything! And consider the responsibility, the importance and the pure joy and love and glory . . . May I use that word glory? . . . Of the chance to be a part of this. It is nothing extraordinary in that it has oh, oh dear . . . it is just as it is, and here you are within a more powerful point of time for the energies that you have been sending are coming from future to link with you, yes.

So be the highest you can be to be able to catch it, to pull it into that which is. I say "that which is", for all time is now. It is just where you are within that, which will alter, as to your mind experience fulcrum of that spot, that which you are.

Realise your power. Own it. Be responsible for it, and allow it to grow in love.

Chapter Nine

Circles

People start to come to circle for a variety of reasons, some just want to learn how to develop their natural ability, some have had a set of events which has changed their life and try to make sense of what is happening to them, others are just curious to if there is any truth in what I do. I can't wave my magic to give them an instant connection to the spirit world. If they are serious and work at it, they will achieve results and will progress.

I am a very idle medium and haven't had to learn how to contact the spirit world, I joke with my guides that I must have agreed to do the work I do as long as they made it easy for me, I don't put much work into my development but am always willing to help people to find and use their gifts. I am so proud of the dedication people in circle have to work and achieve so much. We start with quieting the mind through short mediations, sometimes guided and sometimes just learning to switch off the internal chatter in their heads after a busy day. Then through a series of exercises we progress from psychic to lifting to the higher dimensions of the spirit world.

There is no substitute to being in a circle of like-minded people and learning together but if that's not possible for you now, here are a few simple exercises to help put you on your pathway.

To be able to meditate is a good starting point, if the busy mind is chattering non-stop, it's hard for us to even hear the spirit world when they do make contact, that's why I called my first book, Sit still and listen. To train the mind to be still is a matter of practice and dedication, to start with ten minutes a day is long enough. As we learn to sit longer and quieten the busy mind, we may enjoy being in this altered state and sit for longer. A few simple meditations I like to share with the groups are as follows.

The tree meditation

Sit still, tell yourself in your head that you are going to mediate, do a check through your body to see if you are holding any tension anywhere. We tend to hold tension around the neck and shoulders, and also around the mouth, if you feel tense in these areas, make a conscious effort to relax that part of your body. When you feel relaxed concentrate on your breathing, breathing in at your normal rhythm, in and out through your nose, think about the air going into your body, feel the coolness as it enters your nose, allow about five to ten minutes to fully relax.

See yourself on a pathway heading towards a small forest, notice the flowers and any animals which you may see while walking along, you start to see lots of different varieties of trees, oaks, beech, birch, sycamore, holly, hawthorn, every tree you have ever seen is there. Some small, some large. Walk along and allow your hand to feel the trunk of some of the trees. While some are rough and knobbly, others are smooth. Pick one of the trees to work with. See yourself sitting with your back to the tree, imagine you are closing your eyes and blending with the tree. Feel your body growing upwards until your arms are part of the high branches of the tree; your feet go deep into the ground. You have become the tree. From high up here you can see all over the forest, allow yourself to gently sway in the gentle breeze, enjoy the relaxation. Feel the warm sunshine on your branches. Stay here for as long as you want to. If you want to take this meditation a bit deeper you can carry on. See a dark cloud coming over you, the sun is hidden behind the cloud and it starts to rain, feel the rain hitting your leaves and running downwards towards your roots, the wind blows hard and you are blown around in the strong gusts, just as quickly as this rain starts, the clouds move away and the sun shines again once more. When you come back into the full awareness, have a think about which bits you enjoyed and what you didn't like. As the elements and directions are all very meaningful in witchcraft and affect us, you may want to try the following meditation to see which part of your life needs balancing. Try the meditation to find the balance within to see which part of your life may need balancing?

Meditation to find the balance within.

Start by relaxing and following your breathing as we have practised before, let go of any worries and allow any worries and problems to drift away. When you are ready, see yourself sat by a large still pool of water, it's a hot day and the sun is shining. You decide to jump into the water, see yourself jumping and landing with a splash, have a swim about and climb back on to the bank when you are ready. Now allow yourself to lift off from the ground and fly like a kite. (Remember this is a meditation where anything is possible) Follow the thermals like a bird and dip and dive until you're ready to land back on the earth again. Lie on your back and allow your body to sink into the ground, notice the earth, the tree roots, and the stones. Allow yourself to go as deep as you can, even if you reach the centre of the earth, don't worry you are completely safe and can open your eyes at any time to come back into your everyday life. Next we are going to fly like a bird, higher and higher until you are completely above the earth, see the earth below you. Go on further and further heading towards the sun, get as close as you can to the sun, feel the heat from the sun. When you can't get any closer to the sun, allow yourself to gently drift back towards the earth.

So when ready open your eyes and think about the things you did, which bit was hardest for you, jumping in the water? Flying and being tossed around like a kite in the wind? Flying close to the sun? Or, going deep into Mother Earth?

If jumping into the water was hardest, this is a sign your emotions need healing, maybe you need to let go of the past? Or to try to stop worrying about everything? If being tossed around like a kite was hardest, this can mean you need to relax and stop over thinking problems which will make them bigger than they are. Did you dislike sinking into the ground? If so, this can mean you need to work harder on being grounded. Or if you disliked being so close to the sun, it can mean you need to take action and actually get things done instead of thinking about it too long. A simple way of grounding yourself is to imagine your feet are growing roots, the roots go deep into the ground, and this will help you to stay grounded.

Besides a physical body, we also have several subtle bodies and chakras, the scientific explanation of an aura is the electromagnetic force field that surrounds the physical body, and the chakras are energy points that correspond to points on the physical body but are part of the subtle body. These chakras resonate to colour which in turn has an effect on the physical body, there is one chakra under the feet which resonates to black and white and is sometimes called the earth chakra, we have eight others that are widely recognised, recently we have progressed enough to be able to work with higher chakras and energies which we will discuss later. These eight chakras resonate to various colour being black and white (earth chakra), red (root chakra) orange (sacral chakra) yellow (solar plexus chakra) green and pink (heart chakra) Turquoise (thymus chakra) mid blue (throat chakra) Indigo (third eye-brow chakra) violet (crown chakra)

To me Red is energy, power, and getting things done. The negative side of red is anger, greed, stubbornness. So we may crave red when we need a boost of energy but too much red may send our blood pressure up or make us feel angry. It is also the colour of our root chakra which keeps our feet on the floor and keeps us grounded.

Orange has always been my balance colour, to others it may be happiness, calmness or joy. Orange is the colour of the sacral chakra, if this chakra is out of balance it can affect our emotions.

Yellow is the colour of the sun and also is a sunny happy colour, it's the huge solar plexus chakra, when it's too active we can get butterflies, if it's not open enough, we can feel sluggish and tired,

Green is a steady colour, it is the colour of the outside of the heart chakra, and it is often seen around people when they channel healing.

Pink is also a heart chakra colour, this is for self-love, many people can't or don't have love for themselves but have no problem giving love out but find it hard to accept love given to them. If you find self-love difficult, try carrying a rose quartz crystal with you, this will help open your heart chakra.

Turquoise is the colour of the new age, Aquarius, if this is your favourite colour, you are probably a light worker or involved in some spiritual practice already. It can also help to balance our male/female energies

Mid Blue is the colour of the throat chakra, it's for our communication and it's a psychic chakra, if this chakra is blocked a person may have trouble speaking their mind or may swallow their words as if afraid to speak out, if this chakra is blocked then usually the sacral is too, by encouraging someone to speak their truth, it can re-balance the throat and the sacral chakras.

Indigo is the third eye, it opens naturally as people start to develop and helps us when we first start to communicate with spirit.

Purple or violet is the crown chakra and a direct link to spirit; we now are able to work with even higher chakras which we will discuss later on.

Colour is a good starting point to development; our aura is a mass of swirling colours that change as we live our daily lives and with what is going on around us at any particular time, our chakras are energy points that affect the physical body and are part of our subtle energy system. We can take in colour through what we wear, through our eyes and skin and also through what we eat. Have you ever wondered how different colours affect us, why we like some colours and not others? There is no right or wrong answers when working spiritually so if you disagree with the following information, that's fine, you are just being your unique self. Colour can be positive and negative; we tend to crave certain colours to balance our subtle bodies even though we may not be aware of an imbalance.

Write down the following colours and see how each colour makes you feel either positive or negative. Be honest about what the colours mean to you, don't try to be the same as everyone else, we can learn a lot about ourselves this way and it's a great starting point to working spiritually.

RED
ORANGE
YELLOW
GREEN
PINK
TURQUOISE
MID BLUE OR SKY BLUE
DARK BLUE OR INDIGO
PURPLE

So when you have your own list, check it out with the answers below. Remember you are an individual so you may have totally different answers which are fine.

RED, Energy, passion, action, danger, anger.
ORANGE, Calmness, happiness, achievement, peace
YELLOW, Sunny,
TURQUOISE, Spiritual, new age, understanding
GREEN, Nature, healing, balance
PINK, Love, gentleness
MID BLUE, Freedom, clean,
INDIGO, Mystery, Psychic, night-time, safe
VIOLET/PURPLE, Spiritual, Peaceful,

We use what we call "tools" in our development; this can be cards, runes, crystals and much more. These tools are only props to give us confidence while we are learning. A good exercise is phycomentry, when we tune in to an object that a person has carried to imprint their vibration on it. What you may feel from the object is emotions, or feelings. As we all work differently, some may see pictures in their mind's eye. Others will feel more. Get used to feeling changes in your own body as you tune into the object. Does the item in your hand feel light or heavy? If it feels light, it might show that it has a happy memory attached to it, if it feels heavy, it may have negative memories or a sad memory attached to it? You will be surprised just how much you can get from just holding an object. As you progress, you will be amazed just how much you will get and will be able to give a good reading from it.

The first three questions I get asked are usually, what colours are in my aura, who is my spirit guide and what are the lottery numbers? I can't give you the lottery numbers but can help you to get the other two answers! To practise seeing auras, I suggest you first try with a large healthy tree, look at it in the sunshine, as you gaze at it, you will eventually see a hazy area around the tree, its subtle so allow your gaze to go soft, as if your eyes are looking just beyond the tree. When you can do this, you are well on the way to seeing Peoples auras. Most people can learn to see the etheric band around the body; it follows the shape of the body and is a usually about 3-6 inches wide, its hazy or white. While you are learning, try to sit in low lighting and either look at yourself in a mirror, or have a friend sitting opposite you. It's good to have a candle on a table between you, look at the candle for about one minute, then quickly look up at the person opposite to you, for a split second, you may see the persons aura. Once you have managed this once, your conscious mind will believe it possible which will then allow you to believe it and find it easier. If you find this too difficult, try having someone sat opposite to you in low lighting, look at them for about 30 seconds, then close your eyes, and sense what colours you think are around that person. Use the chart you made to see what you think these colours mean? Have a go, its fun and you will soon get more confidence.

Another way to practice your psychic development is to make some cards, cut some card or paper into about 3 inch squares, draw some symbols on them, such as squares, stars, circles, crosses, make them in different colours. Then mix them up, have them blank side to you and turn them over as you deal them out. See if you can "know" what the next colour or shape will be? Practice and see how accurate you are.

Lots of people buy tarot or a different set of cards, they come with a book of meanings, I have found that although the meanings can be useful, it's much better to see what the cards mean to you, this may be totally different from the meaning in the booklet but it's all about trusting that your message is coming from spirit. Look carefully at the card you are working with, what jumps out at you? Is there anything that kick starts your emotions; do you feel positive about this card? Describe how it makes you feel, what does the picture say? Look for symbols of what's happening on it. Is it an action card, or a warning, or even an answer to a question? There is no right or wrong answers, remember cards are just tools; it's what you get from the tool that is important.

Wax divination is another way of practising these spiritual messages and how we perceive them.

Have a bowl of cold water, light some tee lights or candles, ask for a message from spirit and drop the melted wax from the top of the candle into the water. What shape does it form? What does that shape mean to you? If the shape made from the wax stays still, the answer may be that the time isn't yet right for whatever you asked, if it floats to the side, it usually means things will happen quickly.

On a similar theme, have a piece of card about 10x8 size, fold it in half, have some children's liquid paint and drop some spots or squiggles on one side of the card, when you are sure you have enough paint on, fold the card and carefully open it up, see the shape and colour it forms. Again, what does the shape mean to you; see if you can make a message from it.

After we are used to working with our psychic, we can move onto spirit guides. A spirit guide is a positive entity that has had many lives on earth but this time has chosen not to incarnate, a pact was made many years before you incarnated, and your spirit guides chose to walk beside you. Of course as soon as we are born into the chosen body, we forget all about our spirit guides. So don't worry if it takes a while to re connect to their energy? One of the first things people want to know more about is Spirit Guides, we all have them, and sadly some people go through the whole of their life without ever being aware that they are there. I asked spirit to give me some words to describe a Spirit Guide, they said;

Spirit guides

A spirit guide is a positive entity who is here to help and guide you through your life on earth. They are usually part of a past life and can change throughout your life or can stay with you throughout your life. It is usual to have more than one, five is usual. Most people go through life not even knowing of their existence, but when people start to develop their spiritual life the first thing they want to learn about is spirit guides.

They are not allowed to interfere with our journey on earth, but communicating with them can be very useful to help us make the right decisions especially in times of crisis.

Sometimes when our life changes dramatically we can feel unsure and a little lost, sometimes this is when we are also having a change of guide; it takes us a little while to "tune" into their energy.

One of the easiest ways for a guide to contact us is in Sleep State, when we have switched off our conscious mind and allow them to come to us via dreams. If we are unsure or have to make a decision we are having trouble with, it can help to ask your guide just before going to sleep to help us. When we wake in the morning usually we have a clear idea of what we should do.

Another way to contact the guides is to meditate. This takes a bit of time and dedication but is well worth the effort.

Once we have a connection with our guides they can help us with our everyday life just as a friend would

Some of the things they can help with are

Guide you in your spiritual life

Help bring about balance in times of trouble

Help us to reconnect with our loved ones who have passed over.

Art, music, poetry and creative writing.

Before you start to contact your guide it is important that you are in a settled state of mind, and ready to develop spiritually. If not then it could cause yourself some anxiety and fears. If you don't feel ready, please say so and meditate at home as often as possible until you feel more balanced.

HELPERS and inspirers

These are like guides but are here to help us with what we doing at this precise time in our life, such as if we take up a new skill.

DOORKEEPER

This is our protector; they stop any negative entities from attaching themselves to us while we might be out of the body during a meditation or trance. Unfortunately they cannot help us if we choose to abuse our bodies with drugs when we are not in control of our self.

Chapter Ten
We approach 21.12.2012 at last

Time was still whizzing on and soon it was 12.12.12, this was a very special date and the most powerful portal was supposed to open at noon on this day. I decided to go to a local landmark with Roger, the Ley lines are very powerful in this spot, and I thought it was perfect to welcome in this energy. I was surprised to see two members of circle there as well and as noon approached we all stood still and linked in to the energies in our own way.

Yule is celebrated on 21st December, so not only was it Yule, it was also 21.12 12, the day we had waited for so long. I had organised a small party for Yule and to welcome in Aquarius. Nothing spectacular happened and I think after so long a wait, it was a bit of an anti-climax to us all. We all went home, saying that we would all meet up again in January after the normal three week break for Yule and Christmas.

I woke up on December 22nd and thought I was in the wrong body, I felt numb and totally disconnected. The feeling didn't go away, and I didn't see or speak to anyone from the spirit world all day, not even my guides. When I woke up the next day, I thought everything was back to normal, I could see my guides standing close by, and I didn't feel as if I wanted to speak to them and even doubted their very existence. This was a horrible feeling that I wished would go away.

Yule and then Christmas came and went, I still felt totally disconnected from everyone alive and dead. There was no church meetings until early January and no circles either. I was pleased about this because I had made my mind up that I wasn't going to church any more as I had lost my faith, and certainly wasn't going to teach people about the spirit world, as I was having serious doubts about anything and everything. I had no interest in anything, didn't want to go anywhere, didn't want to speak to any one and just walked the dogs and stayed home. Throughout these few weeks, my guides stood close by, but said nothing.

Two days before circle was about to start again, I lay in bed thinking how to get in touch with everyone to tell them I had finished running all of the circles and to try to find someone else to help them. It was with a heavy heart that I went to sleep that night.

The next day the dogs woke me up early and as I got out of bed to take them outside, I noticed everything looked bright and sunny even though it was dark outside; my guides were smiling and speaking all to me all at the same time. YES everything was back to normal; I couldn't wait to see all of my friends again tomorrow at circle.

As the year unfolded, more and more people told me they were starting to question their beliefs and that they didn't know what they believed in any longer. As I had been through this myself, the advice I could give was to wait a while, don't be hasty as in a few weeks they may feel differently. It's very strange that most of the spiritual people I know have had this feeling of being lost and disconnected. We had such high hopes for 21.12.12 and it seemed things were a lot worse not better! The next twelve months rolled by with the usual highs and lows. During this year earth suffered many disasters such as earthquakes, volcano's floods and droughts, a lot more than usual. The circles worked hard sending out love and light to the earth. At one point we collected lots of quartz crystals and sent them to Japan to try to combat the radioactivity around their waters from the nuclear disaster caused by the earthquakes. Another time I took a bottle of water that each circle member had blessed with love light and healing, I poured this into the ocean and asked that the water would carry our healing thoughts into the oceans of the world.

I wondered if 2014 would be better.

Things got very bizarre in 2014, time seemed either very fast or very slow with the occasional "normal service has resumed"! I suppose like everyone else I got used to this. I had to remind myself to stay positive and not to dwell on anything negative as it would start to manifest as soon as the thought was in my mind.

Sleeping patterns were still not any better; I would feel so tired but as soon as my head touched the pillow, Zing, wide awake for hours. On the many nights that this happens

I don't lie in bed any longer, I tend to get up and either read or play around on the computer. When sleep finally arrives so do the strange dreams, in some I was searching for something but had no idea what? Several nights I found myself working with a friend, we were both searching for something? One night we were rescuing people from floods and when we pulled them out of the water; it was nothing more than a set of clothes. Strangely enough this friend also had dreams when we were working together on the astral as well. Lots of people were having these vivid dreams and all complained of waking up feeling more tired than before they went to bed. The spirit world told me that we were working on the astral in our sleep and that we could ask to be allowed to sleep in a safe place occasionally to rest the physical body.

More people seemed to be suffering from what we had called the Shambhala symptoms which included, Migraine type headaches that didn't respond to medication, symptoms of a cold that never developed but came and went for weeks. Ringing in the ears, dizziness, and the high-pitched noise in the ears. Heart palpitations, feeling as if the body was vibrating, especially at night when trying to relax. Bouts of depression for no reason that lift as quickly as they come. Recently a friend sent me an article she had read about how Valerian and Fenugreek could help to relieve some of these symptoms and just by saying the words would be enough as we can now access the energy of the herb and use it as a vibrational medicine. Hmm hadn't I heard that many years ago?

The food sensitivities came back around now and many people have stopped eating gluten and dairy to try to feel better, we don't seem to need to eat the same foods as we used to, maybe this is because we are changing both physically and spiritually?

Soon the dreams were of being in a vehicle, it could be a car, plane, train, horse and cart even, and the only similarity was there was no driver. I took this to mean we would have to find our own way through this new age as there were no teachers to guide us? We had been given a blank page to manifest the life which we wanted for ourselves.

I was constantly re assured from spirit that I had chosen to be here on earth at this very special time to help her ascend into the higher vibrations, this helped a lot when things got tough which they did very often. It's also reassuring to be able to swap notes with other people in circle who are also experiencing similar things.

Next came waking up with a song in my head, it could be anything, and it would stick all day. I know sometimes the spirit world can pass on a message via the words of a song but this was different, it had no bearing on anything and the words often didn't seem to carry any message just gobbledly gook.

One day I was out shopping and felt a slight dizziness accompanied by a high-pitched noise in one ear, OUCH, I didn't like this; it stopped as quickly as it started. A few days later it happened again, I mentioned it to friends and they too were having the same thing happen. We called this noise downloads and thought it was all part of the ascension process. This lasted between weeks and months gradually getting less intense, other theories are it's to do with the activation of the crystal grid or even the effect on us from solar flares. Many of us were still waking up feeling as if we had no sleep and even had a huge hangover, gradually in time we realised that it's alright to ask spirit to allow us to rest in a safe place to rest and re charge our bodies, that way we will rest and not be working on the astral all night.

Chapter Eleven
Inspired writings from circle

From time to time in circle we have evenings of inspired writings, this is when we each meditate and link to our spirit guides, then ask for some words of wisdom about a particular subject. Recently I thought seeing as things were changing so much, we would ask about the recent changes since 21.12.12, the following writings are from the people who were there that evening. When we hear directly from spirit, sometimes the grammar and punctuation are not correct, we write it exactly how we hear it, so when you read the following words through, please note the phraseology is not how the writer would usually say things. As spirit just makes us aware of the words, it's hard to punctuate writings and the grammar leaves a lot to be desired! I have written it as it was given to me by spirit and my circle friends.

Inspired writings Wednesday circle

Weary traveller rest awhile, come sit beneath this big old tree.

We will speak of times when days were long, and your soul felt light and free.

Oh Lord I cannot sit awhile; I have too much to do.

People to meet and tasks to do, but weary yes I am that's true.

Then rest awhile and share your woes, a trouble shared? Isn't that how the saying goes?

Sleep it evades me, I am so tired, my mind active all night, and by the day I feel so wired.

Each day brings new troubles, more people to help.

No time for enjoyment, no time for myself.

The Lord he sat quietly and uttered no sound, he smiled at me as he slowly sat down,

You came here to help to lend a hand, and now changes have come all over this land,

You don't need to carry so heavy a load,

People are gathering in exactly what they have sowed.

Each soul has the choice to seek guidance within,

To quieten the mind and shut out the din.

My advice to you is carry your own light

Listen to spirit and do what you feel right.

There is no right, there is no wrong

The time isn't here yet when we all sing the same song.

Your progress is destined from your own heart

No set time to finish no set time to start.

All is happening just as it ought

Listen to spirit and harken what's taught

Responsibility for your self is the ultimate test,

To know when to walk and when to take rest

So hold up the banner and shine forth the light,

Let go of the struggle, let go of the fight.

Allow time to see the true beauty of life,

More of the beauty and less of the strife.

Lyn

Hello!

Born a blank page

All children are born innocent, to view the world through the eyes of a child. To learn from others seeing the Mother Earth from which we came from

Connected in a way which is totally simple, rain water, chemicals, yet born to service. We are all born with a book inside us; this book enables us to evaluate what's right and wrong. I call this book, the book inside, not written down, not kept in a vault or a church, but carried within all of us, deep inside. If we sit still and listen, we can see the pages of this book, hear its words, feel its thoughts and use it for the good of everything. May be some of us listen to our book more than others? O some maybe have not yet dusted the cover and turned the first page? My book says to me that to do well is not to cause suffering on any level throughout my life, to respect our Mother Earth and all those up on her. For we are all born from the Mother to experience the physical and with the gift of learning, use our knowledge for all things honest to our being.

Thank you from Russ

<u>*Changes since 2012*</u>

So much has happened since 2012, time passes quickly and we do not always remember what has happened or how it was before that date, but time has no end. All the world seems to be in turmoil, why is this? Are we being tested? We hope for peace and for everyone to tolerate each other's beliefs through talk and connectivity. This seems to be impossible, so much blood and displacement is a reality, why are innocents being made to suffer? We offer love and light to all those who need it, and think of them willing peace. Also for tolerance to replace aggression. We need to connect with like-minded people to find answers on how to help and for peace to overpower the bloody minded, power seeker.

We need help and guidance to make peace a reality. There is strength in numbers, so gathering together with others could be a great force, they will speak words of wisdom to all, and send love and light to all.

AW

The change of time since 2012

A period of time for change, frightening but we greet change with an open mind. In this time we have experienced euphoric happiness, extreme sadness, dizzy heights, horrific lows. The time of such excess's is over and we are starting to find the balance. Emotions, feelings, we see things differently. The lessons are over for all. People have to be more self-responsible for their actions, no one else is involved, and it is theirs and our choices, no one else. If we make a mistake, we do not run to burden someone else. Look at that error of judgement, analyse it, find the cause and put it right. Listen, but again this is a single person's problem or thought. Reflect if you desire, but if not, simply put it to one side and move on.

The men of power will think that their views and opinions are the only ones that matter; alas they are going to be guilty of leading us down a slippery path full of holes. The ordinary man will clear the way, and strength will be gained. The way has been foggy and unclear, but the mist is clearing and our lives are settling, new emotions are becoming easier and clearer to live with. We must respect all; we must walk our pathway knowing that this is our choice, listen to our hearts and live our own lives, not others. Our lives are ours to live, to make what we want of it. Every thought and action is our alone.

Love your fellow man, woman and child, live with honesty and respect for all.

Love and light

Lunar mist x

Ann

Your wings are still in the process of unfolding, and are too delicate to cope with the world – but if you withdraw to a space that is protected, you will feel more secure to allow your heart to give out your love. Your meditation is needed now more than ever as the world's light or rather light workers *lights are needed to ground the purity of the blue ray. The rays are blending as never before, but the atmosphere is clouded and darkness hovers at the edges. Be vigilant and watch yourself so that you do not add to this cloud. It is requiring you to fulfil what you came here to do. This is only partially resolved and we offer you more coverage. It is all about the heart, love that is the most important chakra at this time. As it grows larger, taking on energy because it is no longer important or an issue to stay grounded or connected through the base chakra, as you keep the pure silver thread strong that connects you to Mother Earth. This is also your soul thread, and you are the conduit with your heart in the centre. Allow purer energy to flow, remember bliss and grace are your symbols. By Milly*

For a certainty the effects of the change in this day and age run very much deeper than anyone can know. There is so much below (and above) the line at which most operate. To so many a listing of physical anomalies, or a sighting of rare astrological alignments, or an opening awareness to the inaccuracies to that which they hear, as to that which they feel is of truth and importance is all they consider.

Rarely can they see further than their own perspective, as it is for all upon the earth. That is the purpose of their spiritual connections to their guides and helpers, to lift their awareness from this blinkered earthly perspective. What is key here is love? A higher vibrational resonance is clothing the spheres, a clearer sense of who we are in reality and relative to all other dimensions.

Often those caught up in the changes connect and invest their attention/focus to that which seems awry, not right and in need of fixing. They pin their hopes for a New Dawn to awaken, in which all these anomalies are resolved and dissolved into a purer loving way of living here. They attach still to a future in which this can be. This saddens us somewhat for we wish to again remind you to focus on the now, as the fulcrum to all other dimensions of now—futures and pasts.

Spend more time upon a focus of the highest and best that can be, within and without, for all that you are and know. Disregard that which seems awry or amiss. It has no place, for again we remind you that your thoughts and beliefs, within this fulcrum of now is what is creating your existence for all your future your's (and past ones). Place instead upon that which seems awry a thought, and steadfastly rely upon this to be true, that it is in truth of the highest and best that can be for all that is, for once this highest and best is set with pure intent, it can be of no other.

Let go of your earthly perspective in your attempts to judge and evaluate these changes. It has been ever set that those on Earth have, as a birth right, spirit guides who work with that which is presented to them from the thoughts and beliefs for this co-creation. This is how all lessons are set within the fabric of your lives.

Be of courage and of encouragement to all others who you meet upon your pathway, no matter again of how they seem to be within the roles they are playing out here in this lifetime. Often the lowliest soul is of the purest intent of love.

Grant yourselves permission to relax within this love, to be joyous, to be engaged within a distancing from all which appears so un-right. It is all illusion, the lesson to all of which is of love. Be thus to your highest and best ability. It is enough.

w.b.

Inspired writing by Laura Cooper

It's time to take another breath.

This time it's a new fresher, clearer breath. One with more wisdom and foresight after the trials and tribulations of the recent past.

This time it doesn't feel like a final gulp of air before plunging down deep.

This time it is a deep, cleansing breath. A breath of renewal and rejoicing.

Time is opening up, along with the minds of people. They are realising that all is connected. That we cannot ignore our neighbour for a part of them is also us. So we need to view them with humility and honour their life and essence. To see the light of spirit that lies within them. If we cannot see it in others, especially those whose energy we struggle with, then we cannot hope to fully find the light within us.

This is the next step of loving yourself to love another and to be loved by others.

Recognising that we are all souls and have come from source and will all return to source.

Our journeys are our own. No one journey is the same as another's and yet we are all one, combined, as a whole so we are all taking each other's journeys as we seemingly journey alone.

The best way to help others on their journeys is to be the pathfinder; to show the way.

To shine the light so they can see their way forward.
With each step you take with light in your heart, you will illuminate your way and the path will remain lit for others to follow.

To follow a peaceful way, a way forward with love and light only in their hearts.

Fear is systemic in society and that is how love cannot prevail. By being a beacon of light and a peaceful warrior you can show that fear has little place in this world and that it *certainly won't be allowed to continue to be used as a method of control.*

By telling others what to do or trying to help them by giving them advice all the time, you risk using your own precious energies.

We say again, be the guiding light of peace and love. Then they will see what to do with their lives.

Why should changes of taken place since 2012? Life existence could be viewed as an amazing river slowly making its way to the sea. Its source has not changed. Its journey involves mountains, plains and delta to the sea, has not changed.

It might have changed over 1000's of years, but our time input is meagre by comparison. Year numbers are merely numbers; they could be 1172, 842, 2014 or 4016. The date of entering this life span cold is described as our beginning and when its time is spent, our endings and beginning which one must accept as an opportunity to advance the human condition along its path. Love, empathy and humility could be described as key words as the wheels on our path forward, all the time hoping that it's the same for you as well as for me.

The path that we tread is so often part of the difficulties that lie before us. Who said that it was going to be easy? Nothing is worth achieving if it takes little effort in so doing.

So there we have it, love humility and empathy, words which we forget daily and are aware that we have forgotten them daily. What a conundrum!

Love and Blessings

<u>*Inspired writing 10/14 given to Carol Pearce.*</u>

You ask a complex question of a simple situation. You have still not yet learned just "to be", to exist, to live & explore this earthly realm that has been prepared for you.

In your humanness you seek to understand that which is beyond your world, yet with human understanding. Lift yourself higher to your true self & from that higher plane you will see more and in clarity.

Each speck of light that is life, connects beyond itself to all other lights of life. Together "you" and "we" make a web of connectiveness that keeps the darkness from overwhelming the light. That is why you are a "light worker"!

When you take time to look deep inside the spiritual being that is you, you can see our network, our web of light, love and protection.

Ascension is not to leave the earthly human form & to return to spirit, it is rather a deeper and more clearer spiritual experience while you exist in this dense heavy energy of the Earth.

We your guardians, help you through light workers such as yourself. Each speck of light becomes a beacon of light, of love and hope. When they are linked together, they share their light beyond their own abilities and understanding.

In that connectiveness great things are possible. By changing and increasing the power of that light, that is love, enables us collectively to reach further into ourselves and all beyond ourselves, to touch and reconnect with all that we are and are yet to be. This is made possible through love and only love. When a light shines in the darkness, those who are afraid of the dark can see there is nothing that is to be feared, once your light shines upon it.

The changes that you are experiencing are enabling you all, to illuminate the light that is love, much wider than you ever thought possible. In so doing, there will be those who hid in the darkness, who are now visible to those who want to see. This visibility is causing fear and worry which is unnecessary, for once you see what was hiding in the dark, it is now visible, you can see it and it can see that you are able to see it. Therefore it can no longer hide and you no longer fear it.

Human existence is based in love, yet it has been made and contrived to live in fear. This is not necessary and we are supporting you all, through this time of fear. Once you realise there is nothing to fear and the fearfulness in you fades, you will ascend even further on your spiritual journey. Being afraid of the darkness, keeps you in the darkness.

You were born into the light and may have forgotten that light. You will be required to face that darkness and turn back into the light. This is your journey, that you agreed to travel, it is why you are "you" and why you chose to return to earth at this time.

You came bringing many talents, many you have not yet even unwrapped, there is a time to be brave and fearless, to stand your ground and shine your light into the darkness of fear. Many will run away when they see your light, many will also stay to see what is now illuminated. Those who run away—let them do so, forgive them. Many will return to us in spirit as they are not yet ready for the work needed to be undertaken at this time.

You are brave, you will be afraid of your power to illuminate, do not fear it, this is what you came here to do. To shine your light and guide others.

As your light uncovers that which was hidden, so there will be reactions and some will be difficult, as you first have to shine a light inside yourself, to ensure you are of pure light, this is to enable you to be a true conduit for the light, that is the love. This love is what we are all made from and it is what connects us all, in this world and all the worlds that exist and interconnect.

By unfolding who you are and clearing yourself of the darkness and fears, you will be enabled to illuminate others paths and link into the web that links all things.

Allow pain and fear to pass through you, do not allow it to dwell in or on you. Your own light will heal your pain and darkness.

There are moments you will struggle to experience, trust we will support you and keep your "self" on your journey.

Live in Love and light, allow us to guide you, so you can guide others.

Know all will be well, as you ascend into the higher understandings of love.

Chapter Twelve

Witchcraft in the 21ˢᵗ century

I had always kept my witchcraft life to myself, a sort of private bit that I never shared. Working as a solitary witch, I had no need to join a coven or work with other people. After the popularity of Harry Potter in recent years, I noticed a huge interest in witchcraft, as well as requests from people to help clear negative energies in houses. Time after time I was told that people had bought a book about witchcraft and spells, started dabbling with them, and as they saw no evidence that their spells had worked, they often put the books away and forgot about magic. Some of the books available at that time, were vague about how to work with magic and offered no or little information about protection. So as people were dabbling with the spells without any form of protection and proper knowledge, often they were unknowingly successful, so with just walking away they had opened up a channel for negative energies to enter. Usually this was mild disruption, such as lights turning on and off, objects disappearing and re appearing in a different place, TV's changing channels on their own and light bulbs blowing all the time. A few times it was a lot more serious. I went to one house where the youngsters living there had been drinking, taking drugs and playing with a Ouija board, there were trickles of water running down the walls, but not forming pools on the floor, the water disappeared on contact with the floor, dark red stains had appeared all over the house which, looked like blood. Some of the youngsters had been scratched and had marks on their face and arms, of course they were terrified. After settling down the energies and bringing peace and light back to the house, I warned them about messing about with things that they didn't understand and asked them to take the Ouija board and burn it. Things settled down and I never heard from them again, hopefully it made them realise that some things are best left alone.

I thought long and hard about keeping my witchcraft private and decided to put together a very basic introduction to witchcraft that would help people to understand the basics and the importance of protection and being safe. I feel witchcraft is a way of life, not something to be picked up and put down just at full moon. It's impossible to teach people how I work and my beliefs as it's been part of my life and my family's life for many generations. What I could do though was put together a few things to help people who may want to learn more. When people show an interest in finding out about Witchcraft, I call it picking up the broomstick, it's a time when you know deep inside you that something is calling to you and you want to know more. It's hard to know where to start, so the following information is not written in any context of importance. We celebrate eight Sabats during the year which we call the wheel of the year, and each full moon which in a year we have 13. We celebrate the Male and Female energies as the God and Goddess or Lord and Lady. Being a solitary witch, I don't have to answer to anyone and have no rules to live by as I am in total control of what I believe and how I live my life. One thing I do live to is 'an it harm none, do as you will' this is simple but carries a lot of responsibilities as everything we do has a knock on effect and will usually affect someone in some way. The word witch comes from an old English word of Wiccher, which roughly translates to country dweller. Men and woman are both known as witches and personally I dislike being called a white witch, magic is magic and can be used for good or bad, so be called a white witch to me sounds like we have lost the balance. Although I will add I have rarely had to resort to using any negative magic. I look on the moon as feminine, she has several phases, when she is new, she is the maiden, when she is full she is our Mother, this phase of the moon from new to full is called waxing, after full she wanes until we see no moon in the sky until she appears again as a new moon, and so the cycle starts again. It's not a good idea for beginners to attempt any magic in the few days she isn't visible which we call dark moon, as this time needs special handling and spells cast at this time can go very wrong or simply not work at all. The sun is known as masculine, creating the balance with the moon once again.

The wheel of the year for me ends on 31st October, this festival is known as Samhain pronounced Sow-ain, this is a time of endings, the veil is very thin between worlds at this time, and we think of our ancestors and invite them to join us in our celebrations. This festival has recently become very popular and is a very big occasion in USA even though many know nothing of the roots and why it's all about death. Pumpkins

or turnips are carved and lit by candles, these are placed in the window of the house to help to guide the spirits of your ancestors from the other world back to be with you again on this special night. The Mexicans also celebrate a similar festival on this day which they call the day of the dead.

For me the New Year starts after the full moon after Samhain, so is on a different day each year corresponding with the phase of the moon. Next we celebrate

Yule which is 21st December, this is Winter Solstice and the longest night, the sun God who has been travelling further away from earth will start his journey back towards us after today, this will mean it gets lighter a bit more each day. Living from Winter solstice to Summer Solstice seems perfectly natural to me so I find my spirits lift after Yule as I know the winter is getting shorter. The Goddess of Yule rides a sleigh which is pulled by two deer, if you stop to talk to her deer, she will give you a blessing, and to me this is so similar to the story of Father Christmas.

The wheel turns and soon its Imbolc around February 2nd, Imbolc translates to mean Ewes milk, we decorate our altars with white candles to symbolise the light coming back to Earth. The Goddess waves her wand over the frozen earth to wake her up, and soon we start to see the tiny snowdrops appear bringing a new cycle of growth to the land. This is very much a festival of the hearth and home and to give thanks for the lengthening days.

March 21st is Ostara which is celebrated with symbols of fertility such as eggs and hares; it's not hard to see why it has been taken over by chocolate Easter eggs and the Easter bunny!

One of my favourite festivals is Beltane April 30th; this is also about fertility, hence the maypole which is a phallic symbol. Recently May Day has seen a comeback of celebrating May Day in a lot of towns and villages complete with May poles! To our ancestors, it marked the beginning of summer; the cattle were driven out into the summer pastures. Rituals were performed to protect the cattle, crops and people, and to encourage growth. Special bonfires were lit and their flames, ash and smoke, were thought to have protective powers. People and cattle would walk around the bonfire and sometimes newlyweds would leap over the flames for luck. In households fires were doused and relit from the Beltane fire.

June 21st brings us to Litha, Midsummer solstice, which is the longest day; I always feel that this is the start of the slowing down and our journey towards the winter again. The earth is in full bloom, with the colourful flowers and an abundance of fruits.

Onwards to Lughnasa or lamas on August 1st, our ancestors would be getting the crop of corn in, each would offer some flour to make a hugs loaf of bread as in Lamas (massive loaf) to be shared between the villagers. This is our first harvest.

Our second harvest is September 21st which we call Mabon; a different crop is harvested at this time. Our ancestors would release any high ranking prisoners they had captured at this time, as lean times were ahead, food would be scarce so the prisoners would be traded so they didn't have to feed them. I do a ritual at this time for friends when we meet. We release our prisoners which we may be carrying within. During the year we may have said harsh words or done things we regret. I collect some leaves and dry them, offer these to friends to think about what they may regret during the past 13 moons. When we have thought about anything they want to release, they take a dry leaf and crush it into the cauldron, then we burn all the regrets and get them out of our life so we can learn from them and hopefully not to repeat the things we have regretted.

That brings the wheel back to Samhain.

We also celebrate each full moon, when our lady moon is in the Mother phase, this is a favourable time for any sort of spell. The time of the new moon is a time for new beginnings, a good time for spells which are about new starts, bringing new things into our life. While at waning moon its best to carry out spells to push things out of our life, whether it is, giving up smoking, starting a new diet or indeed finishing a relationship. As a witch living to these Sabat's and moon phases it becomes a way of life. It may seem strange to some people to live from Solstice to Solstice but it's completely right for me!

Did you know that the Christian church still set Easter Sunday to be the first Sunday after the full moon after Ostara?

Chapter Thirteen

I wonder where we will go from here?

So here we are still learning, so much scientific information has come to light this year which supports our beliefs and quantum physics seem to of proven the existence of other dimensions. At the time that I write this we are able to work with many more than the basic eight chakra's of a few years ago. As each person is different and works in their unique way, it's difficult to say to what level we are all working.

Things are changing and I feel sure that even though the world seems ravaged by war, famine and poverty, things will soon change as we settle into the new age, this may take another thirty years, which is a blink of an eye when you think of the universal clock, or the changes experienced over the last hundred years. We went from horse and carts to landing on the moon, every day seems to bring more scientific advancement's and new knowledge. It's certainly exciting times we are in both spiritually and scientifically.

I have recently become very interested in the Solfeggio frequencies and how they can help with our healing, so I am off on another learning curve, maybe we can discuss that at a later date?

We chose to incarnate at a very important time, it's a hard journey but I wouldn't have missed a moment of it.